# 101 Top
# North Island
# Beaches

Also by Marios Gavalas:
*Day Walks of the Coromandel*

# 101 Top North Island Beaches

Marios Gavalas

REED

## Disclaimer

While every effort has been made to ensure the accuracy of information in this book, the author or publisher hold no responsibility for any misadventure that may occur during its use.

Although local advice has been sought wherever possible to describe possible swimming locations, this is not intended to substitute the reader's own research.

Established in 1907, Reed Publishing (NZ) Ltd
is New Zealand's largest book publisher, with over 300 titles in print.

For details on all these books visit our website:
**www.reed.co.nz**

Designed by Vincent Reynolds
Cover designed by Craig Violich
Maps by Nick Keenleyside

Printed in New Zealand

*For Rufus*
*and*
*Eternal Friendship*

# Contents

# Maps

# Preface

*1 01 Top North Island Beaches* is organised into 11 regional chapters, each with an overview. Some stretches of coastline exhibit distinct regional characteristics, so beaches have been grouped according to their similarities. These may not correspond with standard regional boundaries. All the beaches are on the mainland; there are some wonderful beaches on the islands of the Hauraki Gulf and elsewhere, but they have not been included here.

It is beyond the scope of this book to provide detailed listings of accommodation, shops and restaurants. Information has been provided on their existence, but no specifics are given. Contact local tourism authorities for brochures on the region you are visiting.

Where possible, local advice has been sought on swimming conditions. Where information could not be sourced, no details are given. Surf conditions vary with the tide, weather and time of year. Beach profiles and the location of rips, holes and undertows are constantly shifting. Conditions you experience may vary considerably from those given in the individual beach descriptions. The advice is not intended to replace your own research and evaluation of surf conditions. If you are unsure of whether the water is safe to enter, stay out. Where there is no Surf Life Saving patrol, always seek local advice before swimming.

Please read the chapter on safety at the beach. Contact Surf Life Saving New Zealand for the most up-to-date and reliable information on which beaches are patrolled and when.

While it is rewarding for your dog to enjoy the beach, many local councils impose restrictions on where and when dogs are permitted in beach areas. The laws and by-laws are forever changing and it is not possible to provide reliable information. If you are taking your dog on holiday, phone the local council of the region you are visiting for the latest details.

Times quoted for walks are walking times and do not include allowances for stops and distractions along the way. They are provided as a guide only.

While you are enjoying the beach, it is in your care.

Have fun!

# Acknowledgements

Thanks to Keren, who was with me all the way, and 'Betty', our trusty 1971 VW Kombi got us reliably around the loop, in style.

At Reed, Peter Janssen was instrumental in sowing the seed of the idea and Jo Elliott in helping develop the concept. Thank you to my editor, Sam Hill.

The local residents who freely gave enthusiastic advice about their beaches are too numerous to mention. Without their help, the opportunities for recreation, best fishing spots and secret corners of their pieces of paradise could not have been detailed here.

Sandcastle building — the all-time favourite beach activity.

# Introduction

The beach is the ultimate location for relaxation. Nowhere else compares with a beach for the feelings of serenity, calm and joy invoked by the meeting of land and sea. The warmth of a summer morning accompanied by the soothing licks of inviting ocean waves is an image of dreamlike quality, guaranteed to soothe the soul and calm the nerves. A wild, raw and windswept beach produces a sense of wonder and awe, a place to unshackle the burdens of life and uplift the spirit.

The North Island provides a sumptuous combination of both qualities. The east coast and west coast display differing characteristics, one influenced by the Pacific's mighty moods, the other dominated by the Tasman's steady breath. The east coast beaches tend to be furnished with golden sand, while the predominantly black sands create a mystical environment on the west coast.

Each region exhibits a distinct flavour and character to its beaches. Northland undoubtedly reigns as the region most endowed with sandy beaches, including the majestic sweep of the world-famous Ninety Mile Beach. Greater Auckland has by marked contrast the intimate, cosy Waitemata beaches on the east coast and awe-inspiring, majestic black sand beaches on the west. Coromandel's golden enclaves are flanked by green forested headlands and crimson pohutukawa.

The Bay of Plenty is one long curve of sand, broken occasionally by rivers or headlands. The Gisborne and East Cape region is studded with isolated and little-known gems, a character continued through Hawke's Bay. The volatile Wairarapa coastline is shadowed by moody cliffs and often tumultuous seas.

Rounding the rocky southern tip of the North Island near Wellington, the Kapiti Coast and the Wanganui/Manawatu region return to a sandy arc. North of the Whanganui River the characteristic black sands commence and continue around the semi-circular Taranaki coast, a Mecca for surfers. The tempestuous coast of the Waikato and King Country produces some unlikely havens.

This necklace of jewels awaits your discovery.

During the Victorian era in New Zealand, the beach was traditionally viewed as a place to picnic or promenade. The water was looked at but certainly not swum in. Beach attire reflected the conservative dogma: men wore suits and hats, while women carried parasols and paraded in wholly inappropriate flowing dresses.

From the 1920s, a change in social attitudes towards leisure activities and the mixing of partially clad men and women in public places fostered the birth of bathing as an accepted recreational activity. The mild and warm climate, coupled with the physical proximity of the population to a wealth of fine beaches, allowed New Zealanders to celebrate and enjoy the freedom of the beach.

With the advent of Surf Life Saving clubs, scanty beach wear and greater mobility, the beach became *the* destination for courting, family outings and relaxation. The Kiwi bach was born.

For New Zealanders, holidaying at the country's beaches has embedded into the national psyche a proud appreciation of their scenic splendour. Memories of the beach are happy, carefree and nourishing for the soul. It's a formula we wish to perpetuate. A family holiday to the beach is an annual event, a prize for being a New Zealander. Enjoy!

Even on days when the weather is inclement, beaches are still full of wonder and awe.

# At the Beach

The sight of brilliant sunshine glinting from the ripples of water, or a curtain of sea spray being drawn up a coastal cliff by the ocean's breath.

The smell of ocean air carried on the breeze, or the unmistakable odour of marine detritus, collected by the tide into lines of jumbled flotsam and jetsam.

The sounds of excited children playing in the rolling surf, or the thunderous roar of a titanic wave on the rocky shore.

The feel of warm sand welling up between your toes, or the blast of fresh invigorating sea air welling water from your eyes.

The taste of encrusted salt on lips or sand in a picnic sandwich. Fish and chips or ice-cream by the sea.

The beach is a joyous frenzy for the senses.

You can run, walk or stroll, stopping frequently to examine the ejected bounty of the water. Search for a twisted piece of driftwood or a collection of colourful shells.

Swim, boogie-board, surf, windsurf, kite surf, paddle, kayak, splash and play in the water. Snorkel or dive in the other-worldliness of the blue ocean.

Surfcast, fish from the rocks, kite fish, gather shellfish, explore rock pools. Watch gulls swooping, gannets and terns diving, oystercatchers feeding. Observe starfish creeping, sand hoppers jumping and globules of plankton froth skimming across the sand.

Bring a kite, bat and ball, cricket bat, rugby or soccer ball, frisbee, or bucket and spade. The sand is a playground for all.

If this all sounds too strenuous, smother your body with sun cream, put on your hat, find some shade, roll out your towel and relax …

# Safety at the Beach

## Water Safety

Although the water can be enjoyable, it can also be a life taker.

Always swim between the flags. Not all beaches in the North Island are patrolled by lifeguards. Most are only patrolled during busy periods and there are no rules to the dates beaches have lifeguards present. You should contact Surf Life Saving New Zealand for the most reliable information on the beaches you intend visiting. They have offices in Auckland, Tauranga, Gisborne, Napier, Wellington, Palmerston North and New Plymouth. Their website is a useful source of information (see contact details p. 27).

Seasonal Surf Life Saving patrols may be present and not described in this book. Similarly a beach may have a patrol which isn't operating when you are visiting. Where possible, the guidance for swimming at a particular beach in this book is based on local advice. This should always be sought before entering the water so that you can be more certain of the current conditions of the beach you are visiting.

It is a good idea to develop a greater awareness of surf conditions, as this can help you avoid possible tragedy. The details outlined here are given as a guide only.

## Safety in the Sun

Overexposure to ultraviolet (UV) light from the New Zealand sun can damage your skin and lead to skin cancer. Tanning is your skin's response to UV light, but does not prevent the development of skin cancer, which may take 20 years to develop. Most people receive 80 percent of their lifetime exposure to the sun by 18 years of age, so it is especially important to protect your children.

The level of UV light is higher today than it was 50 or 100 years ago, because of the reduction of ozone in the earth's atmosphere (the ozone hole). Ozone serves as a filter to screen out and reduce the amount of UV light that we are exposed to. With less atmospheric ozone, a higher level of UV light reaches New Zealand, with pollutants from northern hemisphere countries manifesting in depleted ozone in Antarctic regions. Summer levels are higher than those during winter time.

To help reduce the risk of sunburn and skin cancer, you should:

- Minimise your exposure to the sun between the hours of 10 a.m. and 3 p.m., especially at midday
- Apply sun cream, with SPF-15 or higher, to all areas of the body exposed to the sun.
- Reapply sun cream every two hours, after swimming or perspiring. Cloudy days still pose a danger from UV light.
- Wear light clothing that covers your body and shades your face. A hat should provide shade for both the face and back of the neck.
- Protect your children. Keep them from excessive sun exposure and apply sun cream liberally and frequently. Children under six months old should be completely sheltered from exposure to the sun. You should seek professional advice on appropriate sun creams.

The lure of rippling waters — fun to play in but also dangerous. Always swim between the flags and be surf safe.

# The Beach Environment

The only constant of the coastal environment is change. The ebb and flow of the tides, the ceaseless clawing of the waves and the exposure to salt, wind and rain create harsh and fragile conditions for coastal inhabitants. Where water and land meet a large variety of landforms is created. Muddy estuaries are guarded by exposed sandspits, sheer cliffs tumble to frothing waters and rocky promontories enclose sandy coves.

From the low tide mark to the top of windswept dunes a variety of ecosystems exists in distinct bands. Animal and plant communities thrive, each adapted to the particular conditions of the shoreline they live in.

In the tidal zone, especially on rocky headlands and stony beaches, the upper limit of species is dependent upon their tolerance to physical factors such as heat, weather and desiccation. The lower limit is related to competition for space and food from other organisms. Many rocky outcrops on North Island beaches display an attractive zonation of species that may include beds of seaweeds and racks of mussels, oysters and barnacles. Brigades of mobile coastal residents, such as crabs, scurry between rock pools, while snails, chitons, limpets and periwinkles shelter in crevices.

On the sandy shore, most species bury themselves in the soft substrate to conceal themselves from predatory eyes. Bivalves such as pipi, tuatua and toheroa burrow into the sand and feed on algae deposited by the outgoing tide.

Flanking the upper reaches of most sandy North Island beaches are hummocky dunes, encrusted with communities of plants. During calm conditions and prevailing onshore winds, onshore movement of sand establishes an embryonic dune. Surface vegetation captures this sand and builds it into a more formidable structure. When storm events occur, the dunes may be severely eroded and significant quantities of sand may be deposited as offshore storm bars. These form a reservoir of sand which is slowly redeposited on the beach to replenish lost stocks.

Dunes are the land's first line of defence against the ravages of wind and wave. They protect the coast from erosion and flooding. Native sand-binding plants such as spinifex and pingao, along with introduced marram grass have the ability to grow through accumulations of wind-blown sand.

They thus form and build the dunes. When they die, they provide humus to the soil and secondary communities of plants such as pohuehue, sand coprosma and taupata evolve. This assemblage of plants binds the dunes.

If sand-trapping and sand-binding dune vegetation is not present, sand will be blown inland and lost from the beach/dune system. Severe storms can cause coastal flooding of farmland and property, and ultimately may cause the beach to become unusable for future generations.

A healthy dune means a healthy beach. While visiting North Island beaches, you should:

- Surf the waves, not the dunes.
- Use accessways provided and avoid trampling on coastal plants.
- Refrain from using any sort of vehicle on dune areas.

Above the beaches are the avian coastal residents. The ubiquitous red-billed gulls and black-backed gulls are notorious scavengers and loiter around decaying matter on the strandline in boisterous gangs. Meanwhile at a discreet distance, variable oystercatchers scurry shyly in search of buried prey. Flocks of pied stilts and black shags may congregate around river mouths, while out to sea terns and Australasian gannets dive acrobatically for fish.

Around northern North Island beaches, rare species such as the New Zealand dotterel use the beaches, dune areas and river mouths to breed. They lay camouflaged eggs, which are under threat from cats, stoats,

Dunes are the land's first line of defence against the sea. They should be treated with care.

motorbikes, 4WDs, feet and dogs. Where dotterel are present, keep dogs, vehicles and boats off beaches.

The coastal environment is the most fragile of New Zealand's ecosystems and the most prone to disturbance. While the beaches are there to be enjoyed by everyone, considerate use and a respect for their unique environment will ensure they are intact and healthy for future generations to enjoy.

## Wave Watch — A guide to reading the sea at surf beaches

### What is a wave?
A wave is a body of water (swell) moving along the surface of the ocean.

### What causes surf?
Wind and storms at sea form pressure differences on the ocean surface. As these undulations travel thousands of miles they gather together to form swells. As the swell approaches the land, the sea bottom becomes shallower, the waves become higher and narrower, and the distance between them becomes shorter. The wave becomes higher until it collapses and topples over. This is *surf*.

## Types of Wave

### Plunging Wave or Dumper
Dumping waves break suddenly with tremendous power, making them dangerous for swimmers and surfers. Dumping waves that break on the beach are called shorebreaks. Serious injuries can result from dumpers violently throwing swimmers on to the sand.

### Spilling Waves
This type of wave occurs when the crest (or top) of the wave tumbles down the face (or front) of the wave. These waves are good for swimmers and board riders. Tubes or tunnels often form at low tide.

### Surging Waves
A surging wave may never break as it approaches the beach. This is because of very deep water beneath the wave. These waves often occur around rocks.

## Effect of Tide on Waves

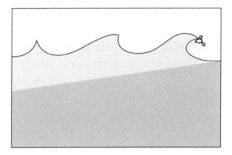

When the tide is high, there will be less beach than at low tide because the water level is higher. As the tide changes, the beach profile may also change.

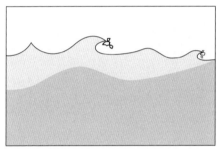

At this beach there will be more spilling waves at high tide. When the tide goes out, and there is less water covering the sand bar, the waves will start dumping on the sand bar due to the steepness of the sand bottom.

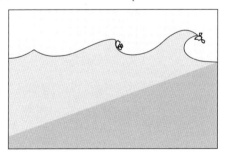

At this beach, the waves will be spilling at low tide. When the tide comes in and the waves hit the steep sandy rise, they will start dumping. This is commonly called a shorebreak.

## How do I Escape from a Rip?

The most important thing to remember if caught in a rip is *don't panic – go with the flow.*
1. Swim towards the nearest breaking waves where the bottom is shallower.
2. Signal for assistance and remain floating.

### Where should I swim?
You should swim where the waves are breaking evenly – that is the safest part of the beach.

### What is a hole?
A hole is where the rip has scoured away the sandy bottom leaving deeper water.

### Where's that water taking you?
1. The feeder current for the rip is the sort of place where swimmers mistakenly enter the water.
2. This feeder current carries you into the 'mouth' of the rip. This is where a swimmer would be taken if caught.
3. The 'mouth' becomes the 'neck' of the rip, and swimmers are carried further out to sea towards the 'head' of the rip.
4. The rips loses momentum as it reaches deeper water. From here, swimmers can start making their way back to shore by swimming out of the rip area.

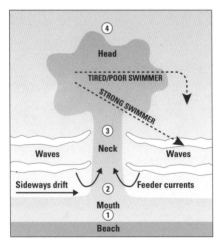

## SurfSafe Guidelines

1. Have an adult watch over you.
2. Listen to advice from lifeguards.
3. Never surf or swim alone.
4. Stay between the flags.
5. If in doubt, stay out.
6. Be sun smart.
7. Learn to recognise rip currents.
8. Always use safe equipment.
9. Never swim or surf when tired and cold.
10. Consider other surf users.

Some beaches such as Ninety Mile Beach and Muriwai Beach are designated highways.

# Signs and flags you should know

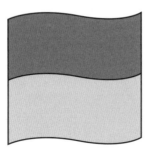

Swim between these flags

No Swimming

DANGER
RIPS

# Contact Details

**Surf Life Saving New Zealand**
PO Box 9205
Wellington
(04) 384 8325
communications@slsnz.org.nz

**Northern Region**
PO Box 2195
Auckland
(09) 303 4303
northern@lifesaving.org.nz

**Bay of Plenty**
PO Box 3182
Greerton, Tauranga
(07) 571 1555
surfbop@xtra.co.nz

**Gisborne**
PO Box 272
Gisborne
(06) 868 9943
slsgisborne@clear.net.nz

**Hawke's Bay**
PO Box 829
Napier
(06) 835 7617

**Taranaki**
PO Box 6019
New Plymouth
(06) 758 2555
taranaki.surf@xtra.co.nz

**Western Districts**
PO Box 28
Palmerston North
(06) 357 5793

**Wellington**
PO Box 9205
Wellington
(04) 384 8325
communications@slsnz.org.nz

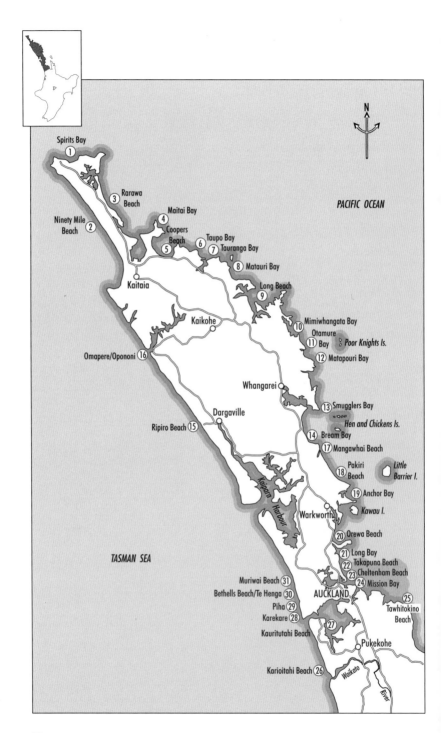

Spirits Bay ①
Rarawa Beach ③
Ninety Mile Beach ②
Maitai Bay ④
Coopers Beach ⑤
Taupo Bay ⑥
Tauranga Bay ⑦
Matauri Bay ⑧
Kaitaia
Long Beach ⑨
Kaikohe
Mimiwhangata Bay ⑩
Otamure Bay ⑪
Poor Knights Is.
Omapere/Opononi ⑯
Matapouri Bay ⑫
Whangarei
Smugglers Bay ⑬
Hen and Chickens Is.
Dargaville
Ripiro Beach ⑮
Bream Bay ⑭
Mangawhai Beach ⑰
Pakiri Beach ⑱
Little Barrier I.
Anchor Bay ⑲
Kawau I.
Warkworth
Orewa Beach ⑳
Long Bay ㉑
Takapuna Beach ㉒
Cheltenham Beach ㉓
Mission Bay ㉔
Muriwai Beach ㉛
Bethells Beach/Te Henga ㉚
Piha ㉙
Karekare ㉘
AUCKLAND
Tawhitokino Beach ㉕
Kauritutahi Beach
Pukekohe
Karioitahi Beach ㉖
㉗
Waikato River

PACIFIC OCEAN

TASMAN SEA

N

# Northland

Northland boasts more beaches than any other region in the North Island. In relation to its area, it exhibits a long coastline ripe for prolonged discovery. The narrow peninsula stretches about 350 km from the Auckland isthmus and is characterised by an indented coastline of drowned river valleys. These now form the plethora of hidden backwaters which make the Northland coast so enjoyable to explore.

At its northern limit, the Aupouri Peninsula offers a character of its own. The brilliant sweep of pristine golden sand at Spirits Bay forms a prelude to the magnificent Ninety Mile Beach, which flanks the western side.

Ninety Mile Beach is New Zealand's most famous beach, steeped in history and shrouded in legend. The hazy highway of sand dissolves into a salt-laden horizon and near its northern reaches huge dunes tower above Te Paki Stream.

On the west coast, the relentless currents of the Tasman Sea have smoothed a shore of even contour and seemingly endless windswept stretches of sand. The wild and deserted sweeps of Ripiro and Ninety Mile Beach are only punctuated by the huge harbours of the Kaipara and Hokianga.

The east coast is studded with innumerable bays, inlets and coves which bejewel a predominantly rocky coastline. Many of the east coast beaches occupy intimate clefts in the craggy and indented coast. The sandy bays are enclosed snugly by rocky headlands, which dwindle to offshore stacks and reefs and are edged with ribbons of white foam. Delightful beaches like Matapouri Bay and Maitai Bay are cosy crescents, while others like Smugglers Bay are more open to the ocean.

Sands of Northland beaches vary from the orange of Tauranga Bay to the pearly white of Rarawa Beach. Soft golden sands adorn most beaches and attract loyal holiday-makers, who often return year after year to their chosen slices of paradise.

The west coast beaches are generally unsafe for swimming, with strong undertows, especially on the outgoing tide. East coast beaches tend to be sheltered and safer. Surfing is popular on both coasts although the west coast offers more reliable conditions.

Kayaking opportunities on the east coast are plentiful, with a lengthy 'feast' of caves, headlands and peninsulas to discover. Many beaches have walks around the headlands, which lead over pa sites to other hidden bays. If you are in need of a change of scenery, it is rarely far to another secluded hideaway.

Northland experiences a mild and equable climate. No part of the peninsula is more than 40 km from the coast, so if conditions are unfavourable it is never far to the opposite coast.

The long history of relaxation at its scenic beaches means most small Northland settlements cater well for holiday-makers and beachgoers. Many still retain an unpretentious charm.

# Spirits Bay

Spirits Bay is the most northern beach of note on the North Island. Its 8 km of pristine sand is the colour of white gold and is backed by low dunes. These shelter a vast wetland, thatched in reeds and rushes and home to paradise ducks and pied shags. The manuka smothered hills of the Te Paki area rise to enclose the bay. There is not a building in sight.

To the east is North Cape and Surville Cliffs. To the west is Cape Reinga, or Ko Te Rerenga Wairua, 'Gateway to the Spirit World'. After travelling Te-Oneroa-a-Tohe (Ninety Mile Beach), departing spirits enter the water through the exposed root of a pohutukawa and make their way to the Three Kings Islands and Hawaiki. This legend is echoed in the naming of 'Spirits Bay'.

Another explanation for the name comes from the great chief of the Aupouri tribe, Tohe, who journeyed down Ninety Mile Beach, naming landmarks along the way. He dreamed that his daughter, who lived beyond Hokianga, was ill and resolved to visit her. He vowed to return, and promised that if he failed in the completion of his dangerous journey, his spirit would return. News of his death was relayed by the servant who accompanied him and the promise of his return was fulfilled by his spirit. Spirits Bay is also referred to as Piwhane Bay.

The Te Paki region was formerly a series of islands, linked to the mainland by a shallow sea. Between five and two million years ago longshore drift and southwesterly winds connected the islands with sand, forming Ninety Mile Beach and Aupouri Peninsula in the process. The former isolation still lingers in the character of the Te Paki area.

A large number of human bones have been unearthed around Spirits Bay, suggesting the area may have been a battleground or burial site. In 1769, when Captain Cook passed, he noted a village on the western hills. You can still see evidence of terraces and hangi pits. In 1772, Marion du Fresne anchored off Spirits Bay and sent parties ashore for water. One ship lost two anchors in a severe storm.

You can climb the hill near the carpark for views along the beach. A nine lb cannon stands on the hilltop. It was acquired by Hongi Keepa from a whaler in the early 1800s and has a chequered history.

For a longer walk you can trudge the entire length of the beach for two hours to the mouth of the Waitahora Stream and return behind the dunes for two hours along an old vehicle track marked with orange posts. This walk is an isolated one and shows the beach and its surroundings in all their majesty.

The safest swimming is in the small lagoon by Waitapu Stream at the northeastern end of the beach by the carpark. This is calm and sheltered. The beach is steeply shelving and is liable to rips and undertows. It is not suitable for swimming.

Surfcasting and kite fishing are popular in the area.

A DoC campground with toilets, water and cold showers is situated behind the beach. It is 15 km from Cape Reinga Road along Te Hapua Road, which turns left into Spirits Bay Road. Bring insect repellent in large quantities, especially in summer, for when the sandflies go to sleep, the large mosquitoes come on shift.

## Ninety Mile Beach

Ninety Mile Beach is the most famous beach in New Zealand, although it is not the longest. Its length is approximately 88 km. When Cook sighted the beach on New Year's Day 1770, he described the barren land as 'the Desart Coast'.

The source of the name is a mystery, but one theory refers to Scott Point, which marks the northern end of the beach. It is named after an early European settler, who grazed sheep near present-day Ahipara, at the southern end of the beach. In autumn, he would drive them up the beach to Scott Point to graze. As he was the only Pakeha man in those days to travel the beach, he was often asked its length. His response of 'Ninety Miles' became commonly used and the misnomer has stuck.

You can walk to Scott Point from the Te Paki Stream carpark, where there are toilets. Follow the stream for one hour and then turn right at the beach. Scott Point is a further one hour and you can climb a wooden staircase there which gives quintessential views down the beach. The distant horizon is claimed by a dense fog of sea spray but the white wave crests sparkle into the receding vista.

Further south are Te Paki Dunes, which rise to over 140 metres on the northern side of the quicksands and reeds of the shallow and sinuous Te Paki Stream. These rolling hills of golden sand are sculpted into ridges by the prevailing westerly winds and have plumes of spindrift curling off their ridges. You can slide down the steep banks on a toboggan in a sport known as dune riding.

Quintessential views of Ninety Mile Beach from Scotts Point at its northern end.

This activity was invented for the backpacker tourist market as another plume in the thrill-seeking cap of a Northland adventurer. The idea has caught on and is now a highlight of any visit to Ninety Mile Beach. If you can't stop in time by using your hands and feet as brakes, then the stream will catch you. Expect to take some of the dunes home with you in your ears, eyelashes and hair.

South of Te Paki Stream is Matapia Island, a rock with a hole, which some say was the anchor stone for Maui's canoe. A seal colony inhabits the island and stragglers sometimes rest on the beach.

Nearby used to live chief Kauparara, who was married to the well-respected and intelligent Riria. However, he became besotted by her sister Kahurangi, whom he wished to marry. In a treacherous plan, he tried to trick Riria into drowning while they were at sea on a fishing trip. She survived after swimming to Matapia Island and gave birth to his two sons, whom she nurtured and educated. They lived on the island until old and strong enough to return to the mainland, then slew their deceitful father.

South of Butlers Stream is the start of the 60,000-acre Aupouri Forest, a huge pine plantation that is separated from the beach by low dunes planted in stabilising marram grass. This forms the backdrop to most of the length of the beach.

On the seaward side, the plentiful plankton is blown from the foaming waves by the wind and coats anything travelling along the beach in a smelly marine crust. The rich waters give life to occasional black-backed gulls, who scavenge on the outgoing tide for any detritus not swept away by the strong tidal scour. The beach is also home to the toheroa, which was exploited to near-extinction and canned near Waipapakauri.

The most accessible place to explore Ninety Mile Beach is from Waipapakauri, which is 17 km from Kaitaia. There is a motor camp near the beach and shops and services at Awanui. Travelling north up SH1 there is a sprinkling of amenities and services, but none close to the beach.

The most southerly access to Ninety Mile Beach is at Ahipara, a small settlement 15 km west of Kaitaia and signposted from the town centre. The vehicle access is signposted along Kaka Street off Takahe Road. Ahipara has a motor camp, campground and shops.

Shipwreck Bay is 2 km further south, a diminutive adjunct to its vast neighbour and separated by a small rocky outcrop. It is signposted along Foreshore Road, which becomes unsealed. Make sure you turn right 800 metres after the seal finishes. The name of the bay comes from the wreck of the *Favourite*, which sank in 1870. At low tide the paddle shaft still protrudes through the sand. At least six other ships are known to have been wrecked on Ninety Mile Beach.

To Maori, Ninety Mile Beach is known as Te-Oneroa-a-Tohe, meaning 'the long beach of Tohe'. According to Maori mythology, a spirit will travel north with a token of its home in hand. This will be deposited at Te Arai Bluff ('Te Arai' meaning 'barrier' or 'sacred place') in the form of twigs, seaweed or a sprig of leaves. The spirit then climbs a high hill called Haumu and bids farewell to the land of the living. It drinks from the stream called Te-wai-o-ngunguru ('Waters of the Underworld') and travels down the exposed root of the legendary pohutukawa at Cape Reinga. From there it travels to the Manawa-Tahi (Three Kings Islands), meaning 'last breath', and on to Hawaiki.

In February each year, the largest fishing contest in the world is held on Ninety Mile Beach. A thousand fishermen each contribute an entry fee for the five-day competition, which helps finance lavish prizes for the heaviest snapper. Kite fishing is popular as the frequent westerly winds are exploited to cast the lines further out to sea. The calm gap between the two lines of breakers (one at the shore, the other approximately 70 metres out) is the most likely place to catch fish. The wider the gap, the better. The last hour of receding tide and first two hours of the incoming tide are when most fish are caught.

The beach has always been used by travellers, as the inland route up the Aupouri Peninsula was boggy and under-developed until the 1930s. Kingsford Smith used Ninety Mile Beach to land his plane after his record-breaking trans-Tasman flight in 1928.

In 1921–22, some 44 contestants took part in motor races held on the beach. In the early 1930s, Norman 'Wizard' Smith, a brilliant driver renowned throughout Australasia for his speed records, attempted a land speed record on Ninety Mile Beach. Local residents pegged out the 17-mile course, but saw attempts hindered by toheroa ripping the tyres and a bumpy surface creating some near-crashes. In January 1932 he broke the 10-mile land speed record.

Today, Ninety Mile Beach is classed as a highway with speed limit signs posted on the Waipapakauri ramp. This is the most popular southern entry point to the beach, although there is 4WD access at Ahipara, 17 km south of the Waipapakauri ramp. Travelling north 20 km there is vehicle access at Hukatere Hill. This is identified by a dome-shaped hill and enters Aupouri Forest. It exits 10 km along an unsealed road to Whalers Road, south of Pukenui.

The Bluff is 50 km north of Waipapakauri and is a private road. This exit should only be used in an emergency and is best suited to 4WDs.

Seventy km north of Waipapakauri is Te Paki Stream, the last exit from the beach. If driving on the stream you should use a low gear, keep moving at a reasonable speed and try to keep to the centre of the bed. Quicksand can quickly bog vehicles.

You should only drive on Ninety Mile Beach three hours after high tide and keep between the high water mark and the sea. Beware of tidal sweeps and high waves which can hide sand holes and cause aquaplaning. Hitting rainwater run-off channels and sand holes can cause cars to flip or an axle to break. Plankton build-up can make the surface very slippery, so you should avoid turning in haste.

The tour buses that depart from Kaitaia or Paihia have a running life of around four years, before they are stripped and rebuilt. They provide the safest means of exploring the beach and will prolong the longevity of your own vehicle.

In mid-March a running and walking contest is held on the beach. This follows in the footsteps of Te Houtaewa, the fastest runner of his day and a prankster. Instead of collecting kumara, as instructed by his mother, he stole from the Te Rarawa people who were living in Ahipara. On being caught in the act, he fled and managed to disperse his pursuers, sprinting up the beach to arrive home in time for a hangi.

Tour coaches ply the vast sands of Ninety Mile Beach and are the best way to see the beach safely, while preserving your own vehicle.

## Rarawa Beach

Even on a cloudy day you will need to wear sunglasses to shield your eyes from the glare of the brilliant silver sands at Rarawa. The sands on this coast, north to the mouth of the Parengarenga Harbour, are the whitest anywhere in New Zealand. They have the highest silica concentration in the world, up to 95 percent. They were mined from the mouth of the Parengarenga Harbour for use in glassmaking. In the early 1970s over 100,000 tonnes per year were extracted by a suction dredge. If lightning strikes the pure silica sand during thunderstorms, the heat can transform it into glass. A star shape on the surface descends to an inverted cone.

The paradisaical beach conjures the feeling of being on an atoll, without the coconut palms. The sand is abrasive and useful for cleaning jewellery. Like the black sand of the west coast beaches, it also sticks to everything.

North of Rarawa, along the western side of Great Exhibition Bay is the long sandspit of Kokota, at the southern jaw of the Parengarenga Harbour. Godwits congregate here around March before embarking on their 11,000 km migration to breeding grounds in Alaska and Siberia. The density of the birds is such that the white sand looks black from a distance.

The shadeless northeast-facing beach has no facilities. The azure waters are flanked by low dunes and the beach stretches 2 km south from Paxton Point. It is generally safe for swimming, although the Rarawa Stream at the southern end is safest for young children.

Surfcasting and balloon fishing in offshore westerlies are popular. The rocky points at either end of the beach are suitable fishing positions. If the west coast is being blown by an onshore wind, then Rarawa can provide more shelter.

The nearest shops and services are at Pukenui. The beach is accessed 4 km along Rarawa Beach Road, and ends at a small parking bay.

## Maitai Bay

The Karikari Peninsula forms a right-angled appendage to Northland's eastern coastline and separates Doubtless Bay from Rangaunu Harbour. Along its eastern side is the lengthy sweep of Tokerau Beach capped by the settlement of Whatuwhiwhi. The last accessible beach, past the extensive peat bogs formerly quarried for kauri gum by the gumdiggers, is Maitai Bay, formerly known as Matai Bay.

The bay is divided into two crescents, divided by Maitai Point, a low knoll which is tapu to the local iwi. Ngati Kura chiefs used to hold meetings on the hill to discuss matters of importance and the well-being of their people. The rocky base of the point is strewn with rocks and fringed with pohutukawa. You can shelter in arboreal caverns and have foliage-framed views of the deeply curving bays.

The various parts of Maitai Bay are known by different names, which are constantly in dispute. The northern bay is known as Ohungahunga Bay, while the southern bay, the larger of the two, is referred to as Waikato Bay. This is further divided into three smaller bays by two short promontories. Both beaches curve around bays with pearl and golden sand bordering the clear turquoise water. Their perfect crescents are backed by dunes, vegetation and low grassy hills. Forested headlands enclose the bays and give shelter from the swell.

The beaches shelve gently and are safe for swimming. Young children can paddle in the calm waters by the sprinkling of rocks around Maitai Point, or row the inflatable dinghy. The boat-launching ramp is at the northern end of Waikato Bay. Fishing is popular from any of the rocky headlands, including those which punctuate Waikato Bay. Snorkelling around any of the rocky points is possible and kayaking around the bay is both sheltered and scenic. Dolphins are known to frequent the area.

By walking along Merita Beach, the first beach of Waikato Bay, past the two promontories to Toroa Stream, you can follow a DoC walk to Whangatupere Bay. The walk is along a narrow marked track, which can be slippery in places. It climbs to Paraawanui Trig, allowing views of Maitai Bay and the Karikari Peninsula, before following the ridge down to the rocky bay at Whangatupere. While Maitai Bay may be busy in summer, you can find a fishing position to yourself here. The return walk takes around three hours from the campground.

The southern end of Waikato Bay has a massive pohutukawa tree which provides ample shade. Rounded boulders lie around the nearby promontory like slumbering marine creatures and create a unique environment in this part of the bay.

A vast DoC campground backs Ohungahunga Bay and has toilets, water and cold water showers. Waikato Bay is accessible by walking from the campground, or following the signpost to the small day-users' carpark. During the solar eclipse of 1965, several small rockets were launched from the bay by an American space investigation team in conjunction with New Zealand scientists.

Maitai Bay is 23 km along Inland Road from SH10 and signposted from the Karikari Peninsula turn-off. This runs into Matai Bay Road (4 km unsealed) after the Whatuwhiwhi turn-off, where the nearest shops are located.

## Coopers Beach

When Captain Cook sailed past Coopers Beach in December 1769, he recognised the area as 'Doubtless a Bay'. The name 'Doubtless Bay' now refers to the picturesque waters bounded on the west by Karikari Peninsula and on the east by the high hills around Whakaangi.

The best views of Coopers Beach, Doubtless Bay and the Karikari Peninsula come from Rangikapiti pa above the eastern end of the beach.

Lazy pohutukawa arch over the sandy shores of Coopers Beach.

Turn into Mill Bay Road then right into Rangikapiti Road, which becomes unsealed. There is a small parking area with a 2-minute-return walk to the summit. Rangikapiti means 'gathered together'. At the foot of the pa is the *Ruakaramea* canoe, which long since turned to stone.

Pa sites at the western end of the beach include Taumarumaru pa and Ohumuhumu pa. Both were once large villages, but little evidence of habitation remains. The inhabitants would have fished the abundant waters and surfcasting is still popular. Rocks at either end of the beach are also good places to fish. ·

At the base of the western headland are the 'Knife Rocks', which are exposed when the sand has been washed away. Maori used the rocks to sharpen tools and formed smooth grooves on the surface.

The beach faces north and is gently shelving with firm golden sand. It is generally safe for swimming with plenty of shade provided by the almost uninterrupted fringe of pohutukawa. The beach used to be the site for rugby matches. During one game a petrified coconut, later thought to be over 25 million years old, was discovered. Running races, horse races, wrestling and golf were all popular activities on the beach for early settlers of the region. Beach games on the wide shelf of sand exposed at low tide are still popular pastimes.

The main beach access is signposted at the dip in SH10, which has a parking area, children's play area and toilets. The beach is also accessible down the wooden walkway from Coopers Drive, where the shops are located. The area has a plentiful supply of motels and bed and breakfasts. Another access at the eastern end is reached by turning into Kupe Road. Turn right into Bremar Avenue, then right into Kotare Drive, where there is a small parking area at the road end. San Marino Drive leads steeply down to a boat ramp from Kotare Drive.

Coopers Beach is 1 km west of Mangonui along SH10, so your fish and chips will still be warm by the time you drive here.

## Taupo Bay

The high cliffs and long spectacular headland at the southern end of Taupo Bay shadow the gentle arc of sand. The bulbous pinnacles are the remains of an ancient mudflow derived from volcanic activity in the region. They provide a dramatic vista from the beach.

Kayakers can explore the holes, caves and tunnels at the base of the cliffs, which form the western jaw of Whangaroa Harbour. The crystal-clear waters around the cliffs and also at the northern headland are popular with snorkellers and divers, for pleasure and food gathering. Fishing from the rocks or beach usually yields some reward.

The 1 km stretch of firm golden sand shelves gently and is most sheltered at the northern end. The surf increases towards the southern end, with boogie-boarders and body surfers spending the most time here. Families often occupy the central portion of the beach. The beach is safe for swimming with few rips. It is a family-oriented beach in an isolated and scenic location.

The campground has cabins and staff can advise on holiday homes for rent in the area. It also serves as the shop, providing takeaways during the busy summer period.

At the northern end is the Taupo Bay Reserve with picnic tables, toilets and a children's play area. The boat ramp is close by and some locals will launch your boat with their tractors.

Taupo Bay is 13 km from SH10, 12 km south of Mangonui. Taupo Bay Road is mostly sealed.

Taupo Bay exhibits the same striking geology as nearby Whangaroa Harbour.

# Tauranga Bay

This sandy beach is nestled near the eastern jaw of Whangaroa Harbour, with its high vertical cliffs and coastline of caves and islands. It is a safe swimming beach and is popular with families.

The beach is good for fishing, especially near the mouth of the Tauranga Stream at the eastern end, and the promontory at the western end. Kayakers make use of the variety of coastal features with many islets, reefs and bays to explore.

The protrusion of rocks, boulders and stones towards the western end separates Tauranga Bay from what is locally known as Butterfly Bay. Take a walk at mid-low tide around the rocks to explore the holes in the rocks and small caves. Butterfly Bay remains serenely isolated from Tauranga Bay.

The 1 km-long, orange sandy beach faces northwest and takes in views of Whangaroa Bay and Stephenson Island. You can see the 'Hole in the Wall' on the opposite side of Whangaroa Bay.

The campground is right on the beach front and has a small shop. There is also a motel in Tauranga Bay, but the nearest services are in Mangonui or Kerikeri. The grass reserve takes up the rest of the beach front and has toilets. The small settlement is tucked behind, on the floor of the steep-sided valley.

The pristine orange sands of Tauranga Bay are bounded by long headlands.

To reach Tauranga Bay, turn off SH10 along Whangaroa Road and turn into Wainui Road. Tauranga Bay is 3 km along Tauranga Bay Road. Alternatively, if coming from the east, take the scenic drive along Matauri Bay Road through Te Ngaire and Wainui bays.

## Matauri Bay

Sitting atop the hill at Matauri Bay is the memorial to Greenpeace's *Rainbow Warrior*, which was on its way to Mururoa to protest against French nuclear testing. In July 1985, while docked at Auckland, it was bombed in an act of terrorism sanctioned by the French Government, killing Greenpeace photographer Fernando Pereira. Two years later, at the request of Ngati Kura, it was towed to the Cavalli Islands and sunk near Motutapere Island, where it now forms a marine reserve and is a popular destination for divers.

The memorial was fashioned by Chris Booth, an environmental sculptor, and is a threaded arch of boulders, symbolising a rainbow. Two hexagonal basalt columns in the centre support the salvaged bronze propeller. A 15-minute walk leads to the summit along a steep track, and affords magnificent views of the Cavalli Islands and Matauri Bay. The start of the track is signposted from the campground.

The 1 km of pink-tinged, east-facing sand is flanked by a long headland and looks out to the wider Bay of Islands and Cape Brett in the far distance. The sand is composed of fragments of broken shell. The beach is backed by a grass bank with a reserve and occasional picnic tables. The bay is generally safe for swimming and shelves gently. Kayaking is popular, especially around the Cavalli Islands. Fishing generally takes place from boats, but the steep hill down to the bay may cause problems for towing.

Matauri Bay lies in a bowl, with sparsely inhabited flats behind the beach. At the southern end is a collection of abandoned cars and rusting caravans, all in their final resting-place. Near the northern end of the beach is *Te Mataatua II* waka, which symbolises the strong Ngati Kura presence in the area. *Te Mataatua* waka was their ancestral canoe and completed its final journey near Matauri Bay. Reverend Samuel Marsden first set foot in New Zealand at Matauri Bay in 1814. At the southern end of the beach is the small Samuel Marsden Memorial Church.

Matauri Bay is signposted 16 km from SH10, 10 km south of Kaeo. It has a store with petrol and a campground. A motel and restaurant are just over the hill at the end of Putataua Bay, where there is a small pebble beach.

# Long Beach, Russell

The Bay of Islands is a snaking coastline of innumerable bays and coves, outlined by headlands, hills and islets capped with lush green vegetation. At the base of the coves lie many secluded and idyllic beaches.

Long Beach faces northeast along Oneroa Bay and curves in a gentle arc around the northern face of the same peninsula as Russell. It is located 1 km from the wharf at Russell along Long Beach Road. A footpath weaves through the town and over the hill. It is easily visited in a day from Paihia.

The shelving sandy beach looks out to the wider Bay of Islands, with Motuarohia, Moturua and Urupukapuka islands in view. Cape Brett recedes into the distant blue and green vista. All manner of sailing vessels, charter boats and tourist craft sail by, while the sheltered waters lap gently to the shore. The beach is generally safe for swimming and shelves gradually.

Long Beach, near Russell, is a good place to escape the summer hype of the Bay of Islands.

In the 1840s Russell had a reputation for lawlessness. Long Beach was used as a location for the reconciliation of arguments. Armed with pistols, 'gentlemen' would perform raucous mediations, with the fracas often resulting in bloodshed.

The Russell suburb of Long Beach dates from the late 1920s, when the first homes were built, and development has continued. The most famous house is the adobe cottage at the northwestern end. It was constructed by Charlotte Preston in the 1940s and is named 'Puawananga' ('the Seed of Knowledge'). A line of homes and baches is now confined by the steep hill behind the beach, which separates this side of the peninsula from the tourist Mecca of summertime Russell.

You can rest and admire the view from the shade of the huge Moreton Bay fig near the small carpark at the northern end of the beach, where there are also toilets.

At mid-low tide you can walk over the rocks to the secluded sandy Waitata Bay, with its fringe of pohutukawa. This beach is sometimes visited by nudists. The owners of Waitata Bay used to keep donkeys, so the bay acquired the nickname 'Donkey Bay'. At the far side of the bay is Temple Bar, a headland which was fortified by the Navy during World War Two. It housed guns and a powerful searchlight.

Kayakers can spend a week exploring the coastline visible from the beach and snorkelling is popular in the clear blue waters. Fishing from either of the rocky promontories at the ends of the beach is possible.

Russell has all the accommodation and services a holiday-maker needs. It can be very busy during peak holiday periods, especially when cruise ships are visiting the bay.

## Mimiwhangata Bay

The beach at Mimiwhangata lies on the sheltered arm of a peninsula, which arcs around Mimiwhangata Bay like a crooked finger.

The beach faces northwest, unlike most of the other beaches in the region, which face east. If the winds are coming from the east, or there is a big swell, then Mimiwhangata remains relatively calm. Its 1.5 km of gently shelving golden sand is encrusted with sporadic shells and pebbles. Low dunes are backed by farmland and the low ridge of the peninsula leads to a hill at the eastern end. The sheltered shallow waters are ideal for young families swimming and the firm flat sand exposed at mid-low tide is good for beach games

The forest-covered hills to the west also form part of the DoC-administered Mimiwhangata Coastal Park. This farm offers public access to the beaches, hills, forests, wetlands and paddocks. You are free to wander around the park and can easily spend a day exploring the tracks to the lookouts.

Cross the small headland at the western end to reach Waikahoa Bay. This beach is equally sheltered but smaller. The intervening headland and rocks at either end of the beaches are prime fishing spots. Snorkelling and diving are also popular.

The views north to Cape Brett are composed of a succession of receding headlands, which reduce to symmetrical offshore stacks. A ring of foaming white water encircles each protruding sliver of land and provides a stunning outlook.

Parking is at the road-end behind Okupe Beach, where there are toilets. To access Mimiwhangata's beach you have to walk 200 metres back along the farm road and turn right after the ranger's house. A signpost indicates the 10-minute walk over the small hill.

Nestled on the sheltered arm of a peninsula, the beach at Mimiwhangata Bay is surrounded by a coastal park.

Okupe Beach is more exposed and shelves more steeply. You can launch your kayak here and explore the numerous headlands, reefs and offshore stacks. It's a short paddle around the headland to Mimiwhangata.

There was a strong Maori presence in the area, with pa at Te Rearea, Taraputa and Kaituna. At times the local population numbered nearly 2000. Te Waero, a Ngapuhi chief, destroyed a fishing net belonging to Ngati Manaia. He was killed for this unforgivable sin, sparking the Battle of Mimiwhangata, which was fought at Kaituna and resulted in a decisive victory for Ngapuhi.

The 7 km drive along Mimiwhangata Road turns off Old Russell Road near Helena Bay. Mimiwhangata Road is narrow, winding and unsealed, and is unsuitable for towing. DoC runs various accommodation facilities at Mimiwhangata Coastal Park. There are no shops or services until you reach Oakura, 15 km away.

## Otamure Bay

The DoC campground behind Otamure Bay helps make it an ideal location for a lengthy stay. The camp has composting toilets and water. You can sleep to the sound of breaking waves and smell the salty air at first breath of the morning.

The beach is approximately 300 metres long, faces north and has rocks at either end. These are good to fish from or snorkel around. The golden sand is verged by a grass strip and a large grove of mature pohutukawa provide ample shade on hot summer days. Swimming is safe in calm conditions. You can set up your windsurfer on the grass area behind the beach or launch your kayak to explore the many offshore stacks and reefs. The intimate rocky coastline is worthy of many outings and you can easily find your own bay in the vicinity.

Vehicle access is at the northern end of the beach from Rockell Road, 2 km from Whananaki.

From the road bridge at the eastern end of the beach you can take a 10-minute one-way walk along a well-formed but steep track to Tauwhara Bay. This climbs over the ridge through Watkin Powell Scenic Reserve. The bronze sandy beach stretches nearly 1 km and has a rocky promontory in the middle, which is impassable at high tide. The beach shelves steeply, so seek local advice before swimming. The rocks at either end are suitable fishing spots and afford views of the weaving coastline. Behind the beach are steep cliffs, encrusted with pohutukawa.

Although seasonal shops may operate in nearby Whananaki, it is best to come well stocked with all you need for your stay.

## Matapouri Bay

Matapouri Bay is a delightful semicircle of golden sand, tightly enclosed by steep vegetated cliffs, which cascade abruptly to the sea. The shelved beach is backed by high dunes and ringed with baches. The only expanse of firm sand is at the northern end at the mouth of the small creek. At this end of the beach, islets capped with hardy coastal plants are surrounded by rocky outcrops, good for fishing from. If you follow the beach around the truncated headland (dodging the breakers at high tide), you reach a series of tiny sandy coves, which lie sheltered with the forest fringing their edges.

At the southern end, the mouth of the mangrove-filled Matapouri Estuary, with its clear blue water, empties into the bay. Kayaking is scenic and sheltered here.

Matapouri Bay was among the most popular picnic destinations during the early times of beach recreation. The sandhills were smothered in lupins in the days before baches were constructed to line the beach front.

As the cliffs around the bay tumble steeply, finding a good fishing spot may take some searching, but surfcasting is always popular. Seek local advice on the best places to snorkel. The waves arc around the headlands to mirror the contours of the bay and are good for surfing and boogieboarding. Seek local advice before swimming, as there are occasional rips.

Matapouri means 'Invisible Place' or 'Hidden Place', and is a testimony to how the encroaching headlands shelter its half-circle of sand. Because the western headland hides Matapouri Bay from the open sea, it was once known as Otito, meaning 'a lie'.

Matapouri Bay is 6 km north of Tutukaka. The main beach access is along Wehiwehi Road, with a small parking area and toilets at the road-end. There is a shop and accommodation in the region.

From the northern end of Matapouri Bay at the low point in the cliffs, you can walk to a gravel beach on the far side of the headland. This is imaginatively named Pebble Bay or Shingly Bay. It used to be covered in brightly coloured stones, but years of opportunistic fossicking have given it a duller hue. A signposted track climbs the headland to a ridge and follows the cliff top, with memorable coastal views to frothing waters at the base of the craggy cliffs.

This walk to Whale Bay takes approximately 30 minutes one-way and is rewarded with an isolated sandy cove, shaded by languid pohutukawa. Steep cliffs, smothered in nikau, karaka and puriri, shelter the bay, which faces west. There are toilets and picnic facilities at Whale Bay, which can also be reached via a 15-minute one-way walk, signposted from the summit of the hill, north of Matapouri Bay.

Whale Bay received its European name during the period of early settlement. A group of Maori saw a large floating object and asked Mr Woolley of nearby Woolleys Bay if they might borrow his telescope. On sighting the remains of a dead whale, all the men of the region rowed out in their canoes and towed it to Whale Bay. Crowds camped on the beach for three weeks, tolerating the powerful stench. Whenever the Woolleys received a visitor asking to borrow milk, the smell accompanied them. The tail bone was eventually given to the Woolleys as a gift, which they used as a fire screen.

## Smugglers Bay

The name Smugglers Bay was given to this hidden cove during the period of early settlement in the Whangarei district. To avoid paying duty on alcohol brought into the port, crafty traders would stash their crates in the dunes and collect them at a later date.

The dunes also give clues to the area's early habitation, with three large middens still visible to the rear of the cove. Ngati Wai and their ancestors Ngati Manaia inhabited the area for centuries and took advantage of the bountiful food resources of the sea. By excavating the remains of the shell heaps, archaeologists have been able to date the shell and bone fragments and deduce their diet.

The headland pa to the west still shows evidence of hangi and food storage pits and terraces on which dwellings were constructed. The track to Busby Head is marked with orange posts and takes about 30 minutes to walk. It can be slippery in places but is well-formed.

To the east of the white sand, the towering forest-covered cliffs of Mount Lion and Bream Head form a spectacular and majestic backdrop to the fine ivory sand. The jagged pinnacles and monumental columns capping the

Fun for all the family at Whangamata.

Sunsets on the west coast are famous, and best enjoyed with a picnic.

Waitete Bay is the only sandy beach on the west coast of the Coromandel Peninsula.

Bound by 'The Reef' and guarded by Castle Rock, Deliverance Cove is a sheltered lagoon.

Dogs love beaches as much as we do.

Dune-riding near Te Paki Stream is a highlight of a trip to Ninety Mile Beach.

The lighthouse at Castle Point majestically guards the beach.

The ivory sands of Maitai Bay impart a tropical feel to the beach.

Back Beach stretches south from the summit of Paritutu.

Even ducks enjoy the sunsets at Piha.

coastal cliffs are remnants of an andesitic volcano that erupted around 21 million years ago.

Smugglers Bay faces south, and the Hen and Chickens Group dominate the horizon. There is limited shade under pohutukawa trees behind the beach. The beach is relatively sheltered and there are fishing opportunities from the rocky coastline near the bay.

To reach Smugglers Bay, turn from Whangarei Heads Road into Urquharts Bay Road and continue to the parking bay at the road-end. Bear left after entering the sometimes muddy farmland and follow the orange posts. The walk takes around 20 minutes.

Smugglers Bay gained its name from the days when crates of liquor were stashed in the dunes to avoid customs duty at the port of Whangarei.

# Bream Bay

Bream Bay forms a large crescent, guarded by the awe-inspiring and jagged pinnacles of Bream Head in the north and the lower cliffs of Bream Tail in the south. A succession of beaches lines the bay, including Langs Beach, Waipu Cove, Uretiti and Ruakaka beaches.

The entire length of Bream Bay is etched with sand bars, which migrate along the shore. Surfers enjoy the breaks in smaller swells on an incoming tide. The best wave-sailing for windsurfers is in a cross-shore northerly or northeasterly.

## Langs Beach

Langs Beach is the southernmost beach of Bream Bay and is a small and snugly proportioned bay. A collection of houses fills the gully behind the low vegetation-clad cliffs. Occasional spreading pohutukawa nestle below the road, which runs above the beach. The sand is tinted orange and rocky outcrops provide good pedestals to fish from.

There is a parking area by the Wairahi Stream with toilets nearby. Near the northern end of the beach is another parking area with picnic tables and a nearby children's playground. The nearest shops and services are at Waipu Cove, 4 km to the north along Cove Road.

## Waipu Cove

The majority of the area behind the golden sandy beach at Waipu Cove is devoted to the Waipu Wildlife Refuge. This stretches 3 km north to the mouth of the Waipu River and separates Bream Bay from a fertile shallow lagoon on its landward side.

Extremely rare fairy tern, of which there are only 30 birds left, New Zealand dotterels and variable oystercatchers all nest in the 128 acres of low-lying sand dunes. The birds lay camouflaged eggs in nests, which are formed from scraped hollows in the sand. They are naturally wary and will abandon their nests after disturbance. Their fragile breeding habitat is fenced off from September to March. Dogs, vehicles, horses and inconsiderate humans can all cause harm to the birds.

The southern end of Waipu Cove has a large roadside parking area, fenced from a shaded grass reserve with picnic tables, barbecues and toilets/changing sheds.

The beach is narrow and enclosed by low dunes that are prone to erosion and periodically fortified with rubble and rocks. The beach can shelve steeply in places, so watch for undertows. This is a fine beach for shell-collecting, with scallops, fanshells and sand dollars in abundance. Fishing is good off the southern rocky headland.

The Surf Life Saving Club is in front of the motor camp and store. Motels are nearby.

The first Scottish settlers, who arrived in 1853, would have trodden the beach. They escaped the Sassenach persecution in Scotland and left Nova Scotia in favour of Australia, but quickly became disillusioned and migrated to New Zealand. The *Gazelle* was the first in a succession of ships to make the journey. Under the strict control of their authoritarian minister, Reverend Norman McLeod, three communities were set up in the region.

## Uretiti Beach

Further north at Uretiti is a DoC campground, which is signposted from SH1, 8 km north of Waipu. The campground has toilets and basic facilities. There is also a parking area for day visitors, with a two-minute walk over dunes to the beach.

The fine white sand is hemmed by steep dunes. This beach is less visited than those nearby, but lacks shade.

The large pointed hills of the Hen and Chickens Group and Bream Head provide the view for surfcasters.

## Ruakaka Beach

Past the mouth of the Ruakaka River are the power station and oil refinery at Marsden Point. Ruakaka Beach is no less attractive than elsewhere in Bream Bay, with low dunes sheltering a narrow beach.

There is a Surf Life Saving Club by Ruakaka Reserve and nearby toilets. Follow the signposts from SH1 along Ruakaka Beach Road. Ruakaka has a campground, motels, shops and services.

The naming of Ruakaka is related to the birth of a great chief. At the moment he entered the world, two kaka flew from the nearby forest and landed at opposite ends of the beach. This formed the boundaries of Ruakaka. ('Rua' means two and 'kaka' is native parrot.)

# Ripiro Beach

Standing sentinel over New Zealand's longest beach is Maunganui Bluff, a gargantuan sheer cliff face of volcanic rock clothed in flax. From Maunganui

Bluff, Ripiro Beach extends south in an unbroken 108 km around Kaipara North Head to Pouto. The distance of the beach varies, according to how far you have to drive around soft spots in the sand.

Swimming is ill-advised all along the beach, especially on the outgoing tide. Strong rips and undertows frequently occur. It seems homeowners in the settlements around Ripiro Beach have a penchant for buoys, which adorn balconies, trees and fences. Keep a lookout for them.

Ripiro Beach is a huge sandspit between the Tasman Sea and Wairoa River. Sediment transported by the Waikato River from the central North Island volcanic zone has been blown north by the prevailing southwesterly winds, forming the Kaipara Harbour and North and South Heads in the process.

The entire length of the beach was once flanked by dune fields, which stretched kilometres inland. The gentle rolling hummocks have now become consolidated with grass for use as pasture, but road cuttings provide glimpses of the underlying strata. A line of low sand cliffs form an apron along the beach, with consecutive belts of dunes and swampland lying further inland.

Any small westerly surf on an incoming mid-high tide works best on Ripiro Beach. Banks form all the way along the beach.

Archaeological evidence shows Maori have lived in the vicinity of the beach for over 1000 years. From the fourteenth century Ngati Whatua inhabited the area and sourced the abundant fish and shellfish.

## Aranga Beach

The northern end of the beach is referred to as Maunganui Bluff Beach or Aranga Beach. It is accessed 6 km along unsealed Aranga Coast Road from SH12. The beach has vehicle access and is a legal highway, although you should seek local advice on sand conditions before driving. There are toilets at the end of Aranga Beach Road.

You can take a walk up Maunganui Bluff from the signpost near the beach. This steep and strenuous two-hour return walk through coastal forest climbs to the 480-metre summit. It commands magnificent views all the way down Ripiro Beach.

## Kai Iwi Lakes

Near the northern end of the beach and signposted from Aranga are the Kai Iwi lakes, jewels of clear deep-blue water with collars of white sand. Dune lakes such as these were once common behind Ripiro Beach before the land was drained for agricultural uses. The lakes have no inlets or outlets, but are formed by depressions in the sand overlying impermeable ironstone pans and are filled from above by rainwater.

The lakes are popular for trout fishing and there is a poorly marked walkway around the northern edge of Lake Taharoa. As the beach is prone to rips and undertows, the Kai Iwi lakes make a good place to swim and paddle, especially for young children. Water skiing is also popular and there are campgrounds on the lake edge.

## Omamari

The next access south is at Omamari, a desolate settlement tucked behind the grass-covered dunes. The narrow entrance to the beach involves the crossing of a narrow shallow creek. Omamari has a toilet and is 9 km south of the turn-off to Kai Iwi lakes. From Dargaville, turn into Babylon Coast Road, 9.5 km north of the town on SH12.

The name Omamari commemorates the wrecking of the *Mamari* waka, south of Maunganui Bluff. The canoe ferried some of the earliest Maori settlers of the Hokianga and Kaipara districts. Around 4.5 km south of Omamari and 8.5 km north of Baylys Beach is a memorial to the first musket used in New Zealand in 1807. This stands in the dunes behind the beach.

## Baylys Beach

Baylys Beach is the main access point to Ripiro Beach and lies 12 km west of Dargaville. The name 'Baylys Beach' is sometimes used to refer to Ripiro Beach. It has a motor camp, café and takeaway and an eclectic collection of brightly painted baches. These hover above the gully, where the road winds down to the beach. Parking is limited except on the beach. There are toilets near the beach entrance.

## Glink's Gully

The most southerly access to the beach is Glink's Gully. Follow signposts from Dargaville to Te Kopuru. Glink's Gully is signposted along West Coast Road, which turns into Redhill Road 4 km before the beach. Turn into Glink's Road 1 km before the beach.

Glink's Gully is a flax-choked cleft in the dunes. The small collection of baches is supplemented with a motor camp, but the only beach access is down a very steep single-lane road. There is no parking except on the beach itself.

### Pouto

Pouto is the most southern point for vehicle access to the beach and lies inside the Kaipara Harbour. In the early 1800s vessels seeking kauri spars frequently visited the Kaipara Harbour and came to grief on the bar. The lack of any navigational point on North Head prompted the construction in 1884 of a kauri lighthouse, which still exists today. It is 7 km from the beach access.

Near the southern end of the beach is a ship graveyard, displaying a selection of the many recorded wrecks that failed to negotiate the treacherous Kaipara Bar. One is thought to be a Portuguese wreck, possibly dating from the fourteenth or fifteenth century. If ever proven, this could have serious consequences for New Zealand's accepted theories of European discovery.

# Omapere and Opononi

Omapere and Opononi run seamlessly together along the outer stretches of the Hokianga Harbour's southern jaw. The harbour beaches are narrow but mostly sandy and more sheltered than their exposed neighbours, which are open to the fury of the Tasman.

Omapere is the westernmost of the two settlements and has a sandy beach accessed by turning into Old Wharf Road, then turning right into Freese Park. There are toilets, a parking area, children's play area and picnic tables. The beach access is signposted 100 metres further down the road.

There are also accessways and picnic tables at Omapere Reserve by the Hokianga Information Centre. Shaded trees and a large grass area are above the beach, while below the gentle waves lick the shore.

Upstairs at the Information Centre staff will gladly show two videos about 'Opo', the friendly dolphin. These 15-minute black and white documentaries bring to life the excitement and razzmatazz surrounding the visits of 'Opo' in the summer of 1955-56.

The bottlenose dolphin would swim into the harbour and play with boats, balls and small children. She possessed an endearing character and charm, and gained such renown that visitors flocked in their thousands to the quiet backwater. She was filmed for millions of American television viewers and accounts of her daily antics were broadcast on British radio. In the days when 'Whale Watch' and 'Swimming with Dolphins' were a distant blip on the radar and humankind's special connection with these marine mammals was barely heard of, 'Opo' caused outpourings of affection.

Opononi still cashes in on its fame of nearly half a century ago with a statue by the motel, shop and takeaway. This is where Opononi's small beach is best accessed.

Some 400 metres west of Omapere, you can turn into Signal Station Road and take a walk around Arai-te-uru. Hokianga's South Head commands fine views of the bar, harbour and high dunes of the North Head. Tradition says that the legendary explorer Kupe left two taniwha, Arai-te-uru and Niua, to guide future returning waka. In 1838, John Martin bought the headland and constructed a signalling mast on the point to help guide ships over the treacherous bar, which has claimed over 20 vessels. His farmhouse was located 3 km away on the hill and was painted white to act as a navigation marker.

The giant dunes of North Head are mainly composed of sandy siliceous material transported from the central North Island volcanic zone by the Waikato River, then blown north by prevailing southwesterly winds.

Both settlements have accommodation, restaurants and services.

'Opo' the friendly dolphin visited Opononi nearly 50 years ago. Her legacy is still remembered fondly.

# Greater Auckland

The Greater Auckland region has the most diverse collection of beaches in close proximity to each other. The character of the west and east coast beaches is most striking, with both providing unique and inspiring atmospheres.

On the west coast the spiritually uplifting and refreshing black sands of Karekare, Piha and Bethells Beach/Te Henga have long been a source of inspiration for Aucklanders. Film-makers, artists and beachgoers recognise the raw majesty of the wild coast, flanked by the densely forested Waitakere Ranges.

The intimate, serene and cosy east-coast beaches of the Waitemata Harbour and Hauraki Gulf counterpoint the west-coast beaches admirably. Tiny indentations in the sandstone cliffs and the shelter of the gulf islands provide ideal locations for rest and relaxation.

Both coasts offer a mixture of activities. The west coast produces some of the finest waves in the country, renowned internationally in surfing circles. The powerful waves, however, make swimming on the coast extremely dangerous and all the beaches have a sorry list of drownings, despite the best efforts of the Surf Life Saving Clubs. You should only swim in patrolled areas and always swim between the flags.

Fishing on the west coast is also dangerous, with rogue waves sweeping the unwary off rock shelves. The high cliffs and headlands have a network of memorable walking tracks, which reach spectacular lookouts. Horse riding and blokarting are popular on the wide, flat, firm sands of Muriwai Beach and Karioitahi.

The east coast is generally safe for bathing, with most beaches offering sheltered waters suitable for enjoyment by young families. Beaches such as Anchor Bay, Long Bay and Kauritutahi are bordered by Regional Parks, administered by Auckland Regional Council. These provide facilities such as barbecue areas and picnic tables, with wide open grass areas nearby for children to play on. Walking and kayaking opportunities abound. The city beaches of Takapuna, Cheltenham and Mission Bay are well frequented and with good reason. Shops, cafés and services are never far away.

With the Auckland region's long history of Maori and European occupation, many beaches exhibit the remains of pa sites and the artefacts of early settlement. The beaches have always been sources of food, routes of communication and sanctuaries for rejuvenation.

# Mangawhai Beach

Mangawhai Beach reaches 10 km from Eyres Point in the south to the mouth of the convoluted Mangawhai Harbour. The tip of the beach forms a narrow spit and lagoon separated by high sand dunes. The isolation provides a haven for rare shorebirds such as the fairy tern and New Zealand dotterel. This section of the beach is not accessible.

North of the harbour mouth the beach continues and is accessible from nearby Mangawhai Heads, which protrude into a wide kink of the harbour. This tranquil backwater comes alive in summer and has shops, restaurants, motels and a campground. The accessible beach area is 2 km from the town centre. Follow Molesworth Road and turn right at the roundabout into Mangawhai Heads Road. Turn left into Wintle Street, which leads to a parking area, Surf Life Saving Club and toilets.

A rocky causeway leads to Sentinel Rock, which is an ideal fishing spot and interesting to kayak around. Jet skiers jump the waves on the bar near the harbour entrance.

The fine golden sand stretches north and is punctuated with rocky outcrops, which peter out to form reefs. High dunes barricade the windswept cliffs behind, which are cloaked in vegetation. Surfers use the east-facing beach on mid-high tide, but being close to the harbour mouth, the banks are notoriously fickle.

The Mangawhai Cliffs Walkway is signposted 30 minutes north along the beach. It crosses farmland and pockets of forest on the cliff top for 1 hour before dropping to the coast. The return along the shore traverses multicoloured rocks dotted with rock pools. From 1 July to 30 September the walkway is closed.

## Eyres Point

Eyres Point marks the southern limit of the beach and forms part of the same headland as Te Arai Point. The Te Arai Point Reserve has ample parking, toilets and picnic tables under shady trees.

The bulbous hummocks of Eyres Point have a network of short tracks around them which lead to hidden coves. The rocks around the point are good fishing spots and the rock pools are full of life. The beach shelves gently to a wide area of exposed sand at low tide. Low dunes flank the beach and give way to pine forest. The Hen and Chickens Group and Bream Head dominate the horizon. To the north, Mangawhai Cliffs form the tail of Bream Bay.

Eyres Point is signposted along Te Arai Road 6 km south of Mangawhai.

# Pakiri Beach

Pakiri Beach is separated from Mangawhai Beach by Te Arai Point at its northern end. For 14 km south to near Goat Island is an uninterrupted beach of golden sand, flanked by private land with no public access.

The main beach access is 2 km from Pakiri and is signposted along Pakiri River Road. The small carpark with toilets leads to low dunes at the mouth of the Pakiri River. A wide fan of fine golden sand radiates from the river mouth and is a suitable place for relaxing. There is little shade.

To fish from rocks, walk south along the beach for 40 minutes to the high cliffs with a rocky reef at their base. Surfcasting is also popular at the mouth of the Pakiri River.

Surfers enjoy the best conditions in an easterly swell around high tide. Pakiri Beach is an ocean beach and prone to rips and undertows. Seek local advice before swimming. The nearby campground has a shop and chalet accommodation.

Pakiri is 10 km from Leigh along Pakiri Road.

## Te Arai Point

Te Arai Point is hard work to get to along pot-holed, metalled roads. From Pakiri, follow Pakiri Road for 2 km and turn right into Rahuikiri Road. Turn right into Pakiri Beach Road and follow the signs for Tomarata. In Tomarata, turn right into School Road, then right into Ocean View Road. Shortly after the junction with Lake Road to Mangawhai, turn right through private forestry land, which leads along Te Arai Road. The road may be closed due to logging activities.

Te Arai Point is a striking headland and the only rock for a considerable distance along the coast. A rock shelf is exposed after high tide and is good for fishing. Surfers make the trip here for the waves on the northern side of the headland. The area is also good for snorkelling. Seek local advice about diving spots.

The sands of Pakiri Beach are derived from the Waikato River, which 6500 years ago plied a course to the east coast and transported sediment from the Taupo region.

The area was formerly known as Pakirikiri. In 1850 the headland at the mouth of the Pakiri River was granted to Te Kiri, an ancestor of Ngati Wai and the hapu Ngati Manuhiri. Middens nearby show the local waters were abundant with shellfish and fish. Inland, logged kauri timber was floated down the Pakiri River to a mill at the river mouth, where a boat-building yard was also situated.

The area has been suction-dredged for sand and up to 200,000 cubic metres per year are removed. There is debate as to how this affects the profile of the beach and its resistance to damage from storms.

## Anchor Bay

The pristine north-facing beaches around Anchor Bay are deeply scalloped and separated by prominent rocky outcrops. There are no buildings behind the beaches and substantial dunes lock the view to the seaward horizon. Little Barrier Island dominates the frame like a sombre monolith. The views along the coast stretch north to Cape Rodney and east along the craggy cliffs towards Tokatu Point.

The long, protruding Tawharanui Peninsula forms the northwestern entrance to the Hauraki Gulf. Its name means the 'abundant edible bracts of the kiekie vine'. The strategic position was occupied by Ngati Raupo when European settlers first arrived in the 1830s.

Tawharanui Regional Park occupies the slender tip of the Tawharanui Peninsula, which separates Omaha Bay from Kawau Bay. Its isolation adds to the fresh and rugged character of its natural splendour.

The 2 km of Anchor Bay are divided into three scallops by Flat Rock and Comet Rock. The easternmost beach nearest to the carpark is the most popular. The two western bays have dune fields behind the shore. Accessways are provided all along the beaches, which are all gently shelving and safe for swimming in calm conditions.

The park has a network of walking tracks that follow rocky coastlines to high lookouts, traverse coastal forests and undulate over windy pasture-covered ridges. A map showing the tracks is posted on the information panel near the carpark.

The park has toilets, picnic tables, barbecues and camping grounds. An information centre provides activities relating to the park's natural history, which are geared towards children's learning.

The area at the north of Anchor Bay is a Marine Protected Area and harbours abundant fish and marine life. The rocks at the eastern end of the bay offer snorkellers a varied and colourful marinescape, and diving is also popular. The taking of any life or objects from the sea is strictly prohibited.

Kayaking around the rocky protrusion at Tokatu Point rewards you with fine views, and the southern rocky coastline of the park provides differing characteristics from those of Anchor Bay.

Tawharanui Regional Park is 14 km from Matakana. It is signposted along Takatu Road from Leigh Road north of Matakana.

The scalloped coves of Anchor Bay are fringed by Tawharanui Regional Park.

# Orewa Beach

Orewa Beach stretches 3 km from the Orewa Reserve at the mouth of the Orewa River to Arundel Reserve by Nukumea Stream at its northern end. It is a sizeable beach with a very wide expanse of sand exposed at low tide. The view from the lookout 500 metres along SH1 north of the town gives the best impression of the vast carpet of sand.

The southern part of the beach is flanked by the spacious Orewa Reserve. The wide grassed area has picnic tables, children's playgrounds and toilets with showers. The Surf Life Saving Club is situated here by the huge parking area. Despite the space, it is always crowded on a hot summer's day.

Further north, access is along Marine View, which has a boat ramp, but no trailer park, Kohu Street, Noel Avenue and Puriri Avenue. There is only limited parking at each access. At the northern end Arundel Place has toilets, although the boat ramp has succumbed to the powers of erosion.

The flat firm sand is good for blokarting, kite flying and ball games. Swimming is generally safe. The shallow waters are warmed by the sun and suitable for paddling and wading, although sometimes the tide can reach to the rock walls, limiting the usable section of the beach.

The Millennium Walkway follows the entire beach from the mouth of the Orewa River north. In parts it enters reserves, but mostly passes by beachfront properties or the shore. A stroll along the beach is just as pleasant. The Moana Reserve opposite the town centre is being developed for recreation.

Orewa has all the accommodation and facilities a holiday-maker needs.

# Long Bay

Bounded at its southern end by striking layered sandstone and siltstone cliffs, and reaching 1 km to the creek at its northern end, Long Bay's attractive setting makes it a popular destination. The entire length of the beach is bordered by Long Bay Regional Park, which is brimming with facilities. Five parking areas, a restaurant, picnic benches, children's play area (with a flying fox), toilets and an environment centre explaining the natural history and life of the area are all within walking distance in the park.

Long Bay Regional Park was established in 1965 and purchased from the Vaughan family, whose original kauri and puriri homestead stands lovingly restored at the road-end. Dormer windows and wide verandahs give enviable viewpoints over Long Bay's golden sand.

The beach shelves gently, exposing a wide shelf of sand. In calm conditions it is generally safe for swimming. Bring footballs, cricket or baseball equipment. There are wide grassed areas close to the carpark behind the beach for setting up windsurfers. Kayaking is popular through the waters of the nearby Marine Reserve. Diving and snorkelling in the shallow waters reveal the regenerating ecosystems.

The Long Bay-Okura Marine Reserve was established in 1995 and protects all the marine life within its boundaries. The sheltered and tranquil waters of the upper Waitemata Harbour exhibit a wide variety of habitats with sandy beaches, rocky reefs, exposed cliffs and mud flats.

North of Long Bay is a walk to the mouth of the Okura River.

From the far side of the creek at the northern end of the beach a coastal walk leads to the Okura River. The walk takes approximately 3 hours return and follows a marked and well-formed track. The first hour to Piripiri Point can be muddy after periods of rain before it descends to the Okura River mouth. Three hours either side of low tide you can continue along the coast to Pohutukawa Bay, which is known for occasional nude bathing.

This pristine coastline is a wave-cut platform of sandstone at the base of stratified cliffs. Oysters, barnacles, periwinkles and whelks cling to the rock surface and chitons shelter in hollows. The barnacle zone provides grip over the slippery algae surface and is a safe distance away from the cliffs.

The Maori name for Long Bay is Oneroa, which means 'long expanse of sand'. The area was successively inhabited by descendants of the Tainui waka and then occupied by Ngati Tai. The bountiful shores provided sustenance and a pa site was built near Piripiri Point.

Long Bay is reached by following Glenvar Road and Beach Road from East Coast Road. Take the Oteha Valley junction from SH1.

## Cheltenham Beach

The best views of Cheltenham Beach are undoubtedly from North Head, at the beach's southeastern corner.

North Head's location at the upper jaw of the entrance to Waitemata Harbour has been utilised in the successive waves of construction of military defences. During the late 1800s, with the fear of a Russian invasion, three forts were built which were later manned during World War One. A shot was never fired in war from North Head. Children can scurry through the tunnels beneath the gun emplacements and run free on the open grassed hill. The 360-degree views of the City, Rangitoto and North Shore stretch to the horizon.

There is a sprinkling of secluded sandy beaches on the coastal section of the walk around North Head. Their golden sand lies beneath pohutukawa, which cling to the layered cliffs behind.

Access to North Head is from the wooden staircase at the southeastern corner of Cheltenham Beach. The gate is open between 6 a.m. and 10 p.m. The volcanic cone erupted in a series of explosions 50,000 years ago. Ngati Paoa and Ngapuhi occupied the strategic site and built pa there.

Cheltenham Beach is a cosy beach with some elegant villas veiled behind twisting pohutukawa branches. A walk over the broken shells and pink-tinged sand takes in views of Rangitoto, which graces the horizon with its attenuated curves.

In 1904, the North Shore Rowing Club held its outing at Cheltenham Beach. Bowler hats and suits were typically worn by the male spectators, while ostrich feathers and long skirts were worn by the women. Because of the beach's easy access from the Devonport ferry, it quickly became a popular destination for beachgoers. Picnicking and promenading were more popular than bathing.

The strip of sand is narrow and scattered with seaweed and shells. Access is at the southeastern end from Macky Avenue off Takarunga Road. To the north, there are access points along Cheltenham Road, where there is a restaurant on the beach front. Balmain Reserve off Oxford Terrace has toilets. Arawa Avenue has a boat ramp and shower.

A shallow shelf extends from the beach and provides sheltered swimming. This is a good beach to visit with a young family.

## Takapuna Beach

Takapuna Beach has long been a playground for Aucklanders. Its wide expanse of firm sand and nearby Lake Pupuke have always attracted sporting events. As early as the 1860s, races were held on the beach. Horse-drawn carriages later became a common sight. Boating was always a regular activity, as the sheltered water of the Rangitoto Channel allowed easy launching in the shallow water. Takapuna had its own boat club in 1920.

Bathing commenced around 1890, but public opinion was against ladies entering the water. Men were expected to wear two-piece costumes that covered flesh from the neck to the knees. Young men who offended by swimming in one-piece costumes from the waist to the knee were usually expelled from the beach. Swimming between the hours of 8 a.m. and 6 p.m. was scorned and bathing during the hours of church on Sunday morning was positively sinful. The pattern of costumes and towels had to be approved by a council inspector, who was responsible for ensuring all conduct on the beach was proper.

Today, Takapuna is a city beach with a wide area of firm golden sand exposed at low tide. Morning joggers exercise their dogs and young families fossick for shells sprinkled on the sand's surface. Pohutukawa lazing on the shoreline frame Rangitoto's gentle profile and are well-spaced, giving them freedom to blossom to their full proportions. Low stunted headlands give Takapuna Beach an open, fresh and welcoming feel. Sea kayakers use the beach for launching and take advantage of the shelter provided by Rangitoto. From the northern end of Takapuna Beach you can rock-hop past the beachfront dwellings to a wide concrete walkway that reaches Milford Beach. This takes around 30 minutes one-way.

From SH1 take the Esmonde Road interchange and turn left at Lake Road. This leads to the city centre and main beach. The main access to the beach is from Gould Reserve off The Strand. There are toilets, picnic tables and benches. Other accessways are from Lake Road, Blomfield Spa, Sanders Avenue, Park Avenue, Rewiti Avenue, Ewen Street and Hauraki Road, where there are also toilets.

Takapuna centre is in close proximity to the northern end of the beach and a campground is situated on the far side of the boat ramp.

### St Leonards Beach

Except in rough conditions, at most tides you can skirt around the narrow southern headland to St Leonards Beach. The resistant beds of sandstone have been sculpted to form shelves, which you can walk over. Be careful on patches of slippery algal film, which coat the wetter areas of rock.

St Leonards Beach is a world away from Takapuna Beach and receives fewer visitors than its busier neighbour. The wide flat shelf of sand is clear of seaweed and is backed by vertical cliffs. The more resistant layers of strata jut on to the beach and are encrusted with mussels and barnacles. Rickety wooden stairways climb to mansions on the high ground behind the beach. The beach is gently shelving and suitable for swimming. The flat profile and shallow waters are warmed intensively by the summer sun.

Access is also from St Leonards Road before Takapuna Grammar School, off Lake Road, south of Takapuna town centre.

# Mission Bay

Mission Bay is the jewel in the crown of the beaches near Auckland City. It is a beach to people-watch and be seen at. A string of trendy cafés lines the footpath. These are the places to drink lattés and observe the world go by.

Morning joggers in lycra parade along the promenade directly behind the beach. In-line skaters weave between the throngs of tourists and city folk. The gently curving form of Rangitoto fills the horizon.

Mission Bay caters well for visitors. At the western end is a carpark with children's play area, barbecues and toilets. Adorning the wide grass reserve behind the beach is the Davis Memorial Fountain, whose four grotesque sea monsters spout water from their mouths. The fountain is lit at night. Changing sheds and more toilets are situated towards the eastern end near another carpark.

The gently shelving arc of golden sand is overlain with shells. Hauraki Gulf waters lap the shore, and shelter from Rangitoto provides safe swimming. The beach's northerly aspect and sheltered location make it warm, except when the 'maragai' or northeasterly gale blows. A flat shelf of sand sits atop the beach and is good for games. However, in summer Mission Bay can be so busy there is standing room only.

The attractive stone Melanesian Mission House at the bay's western end was constructed in 1860 as a college for Pacific Islanders. It was one of New Zealand's first flying schools in the 1920s. Later it became a museum and has now been converted into a restaurant.

## Tawhitokino Beach

Tawhitokino Beach is reached via a 45-minute one-way track from the carpark at Waiti Bay. Cross the colourful headland to the south and fossick through the bountiful rock pools. This headland is only passable three hours either side of low tide and leads to Tuturau Bay.

The views of the entire length of the Coromandel Peninsula are unsurpassed as there are no islands to obstruct the view. A veil of haze shimmers over the waters of the Hauraki Gulf, which change colour with varied weather.

The orange cliffs impart a warm hue to Tuturau Bay, which is an idyllic sheltered sandy cove bordered by pohutukawa. Approximately two-thirds of the way along the beach, just past the bach and creek, a stepped path leads through cool, shaded coastal forest to Tawhitokino Beach. This section of the walk takes 30 minutes and is aided by steps over the sometimes steep headland. The canopy of manuka shelters a vigorously regenerating remnant of coastal forest.

The forest behind the beach provides habitat for many birds, including kingfishers, shining cuckoo and grey warbler. The abundant rock pools on the walk harbour lively microcosms of marine life.

Tawhitokino Beach is a 1.5 km sweep of fine sand framed by coastal forest which merges with its shaded rear margins. The sand is wide enough for beach games and the water is generally safe for swimming. Any of the rocky headlands along the way are suitable for fishing.

To access Tawhitokino Beach from Kawakawa Bay, follow Kawakawa Bay Coast Road for 4.3 km to the carpark at Waiti Bay. There are toilets and picnic tables nearby. There is a beach area close to the carpark, suitable for launching a kayak or setting up a windsurfer.

## Karioitahi Beach

The Awhitu Peninsula juts out for approximately 40 km from the mouth of the Waikato River at its southern margin to Manukau Heads at the entrance to Manukau Harbour. Karioitahi Beach runs along its entire western margin.

During the last one million years, the peninsula has been built up of layers of sand and volcanic ash deposits blown from the south. Near its northern reaches, the ancient dunes are over 300 metres thick. The strong relief and grand scale of the hills provide an awe-inspiring setting behind the beach.

It is thought the Awhitu Peninsula was first settled by the Tainui people, who sheltered their great waka on land before moving with their chief, Hoturoa, to Kawhia.

The wide, firm, flat sands of Karioitahi and the prevalent winds are popular with blokarters.

To reach Karioitahi Beach from Waiuku, turn into Constable Road from near the Information Centre and follow it 8 km along Karioitahi Road to the beach. Where the cliffs break, the carpark fans to the left towards the Surf Life Saving Club. A toilet block with changing sheds is on the right.

Imposing cliffs of sand slump towards the beach and are partially stabilised by flax, which leans inland towards the cliff face. The wind can funnel ferociously through the gap, so hold on to your hat. At the mouth of the small stream is a wide area of firm sand suitable for blokarting. The hard sand is often used for horse-riding. Take the dog for a walk next to the frothing surf and watch the showers pass over the black sand to leave it glistening.

The beach is prone to the onslaught of erosion from the Tasman Sea. Inconsiderate use of 4WDs and beach vehicles may result in access being restricted. Advisory signs are posted at the main beach entrance. Seek local advice before swimming or driving 4WDs along the beach. The cliffs are used by hang-gliders and parapenteurs. Fishing and kite fishing are popular at the mouth of the stream.

Hector's dolphin is the world's smallest and rarest dolphin. A small North Island population inhabits shallow waters between New Plymouth and Hokianga Harbour. They have a rounded dorsal fin and black, white and grey colouring. They have been sighted at Karioitahi. The North Island species is now called Maui's dolphin.

### Hamiltons Gap

The only other beach entrance is at Hamiltons Gap, 20 km north of the Waiuku entrance. Turn left into West Cost Road, 1.8 km north of Pollok. The road drops 3.5 km to a parking area with toilets. Beach access can involve getting wet feet if the creek level is high.

The usable beach area is confined by rocks on both sides, so you will only want to come here for a walk to blow the cobwebs away. The wind howls through the break in the cliffs and rustles the flax leaves in the Waimatuku Reserve.

# Kauritutahi Beach

Weaving indentations skirt the eastern side of Awhitu Peninsula and when the tide is in, these form shallow and sheltered swimming areas such as Kauritutahi Beach. The cosy enclave of white sand is divided by lines of shells, congregated into small ridges by the lapping of Manukau Harbour waves over the tidal mud flats.

The beach is best enjoyed at its southern end, where there is shade from a large pohutukawa tree. The antiquated jetty still sits proud, pointing to Kauritutahi Island. Kauritutahi means 'lone kauri'. Picnic tables and a toilet are situated just below the Brook Homestead. This elegant cottage is perched firmly on solid brick piles in a garden of mature Lawson cypress trees and a huge macrocarpa. The well-preserved kauri cladding was pit-sawn from Orua Bay timber and also lines the interior walls. James and Sarah Brook lived here from 1880 and with their five children farmed the area.

The beach is a five-minute walk from the carpark at Awhitu Regional Park. To reach the southern end of the beach, walk across a mown grass strip that traverses a wetland area. Fernbirds and banded rails sometimes sleek through the reeds and rushes. An emerging kahikatea forest grows at the foot of the rich green hills. As the area is still farmed, dogs should stay at home.

Awhitu Regional Park is 33 km north of Waiuku along Awhitu Road. It has toilets, picnic tables, barbecues and a campground. The drive over the Awhitu Peninsula undulates through steep farming country. The Tasman Sea bounds one side and the expanse of the Manukau Harbour the other.

## Karekare

Karekare is a mystical beach, inspiring wonder and awe in anyone treading its dark sands. Imposing cliffs shrouded in a robe of greenery rise sharply and unabated for 300 metres. Vegetation takes hold only where flat ledges allow.

The Watchman, also known as Te Matua, stands sentinel near the mouth of the Karekare Stream, its razor edge ridge penetrating the ground like a sabre. A broad plateau of fine tanned sand sweeps to the rolling surf and a wall of sea spray is blown incessantly onshore by the ocean's breath.

Karekare is a beach for getting back to basics, a raw and untamed landscape guaranteed to rid the busy mind of clutter. Take a walk around Karekare Point at the southern end of the beach and the vast expanse of swampland stretching to Whatipu opens up. This is a desolate landscape at the northern entrance to Manukau Harbour. Sand dunes, swamps, lagoons and cliffs back the swirling and confused waters.

A sawmill was constructed in 1881 below the nearby Opal Pools and timber and logs were transported along a tramway to Whatipu. Karekare served as a staging-post for logs moved from Piha. Little remains of the trestles or rails, except a 20-metre tunnel about 20 minutes' walk south of Karekare Point.

In 1860 the schooner *Union* was wrecked at the northern end of the bay and for many years after the beach north of The Watchman was known as Union Bay. In 1863 HMS *Orpheus* was wrecked nearby, with the loss of 189 lives.

The original name for Karekare was 'Waikarekare', meaning 'the ripple on the crest of the wave'. A series of breaks run all along the beach and reliable waves are found off the southern and northern ends. These are best suited to experienced surfers. The sand at Karekare is firm and even. Children can ride bicycles and tricycles at mid-low tide. Bring a kite or ball games as the open area is vast and spacious, except during busy summer months.

Horse-riding on the beach invokes a sense of freedom found nowhere else.

As with all west coast beaches, swimming is very dangerous. The Surf Life Saving Club was founded in 1935. Following the rescue of Hazel Bentham by sea plane, the newly formed and penniless club was sent a bill for £40 by the Air Force, a sum that has never been paid.

Fishing off the rocks at the northern headland is possible but dangerous. Seek local advice before venturing here or fish with someone experienced, as many lives have been lost through rogue waves, or being caught by the incoming tide.

Striking views of Karekare are found by following Comans Track. Head up Watchmans Road to where the start of the track is signposted and climb as high as you like. The track is steep but well-formed, and reaches several lookouts where the vegetation has been cleared.

A highlight for horse-riding enthusiasts are the Karekare Races, held in late summer. These are attended by families in a day of fund-raising and fun.

Karekare is signposted off Piha Road along Karekare Road, which is narrow, steep and winding. The small parking area has a few picnic tables and toilets are nearby. The beach is a 5-minute walk from the carpark alongside the Karekare Stream. This is usually ankle deep. It skirts the dunes before opening out to the wild expanse of the beach. Another pleasant accessway is by crossing the bridge over the stream and following the Pohutukawa Glade Walk for 10 minutes. This passes a shady grove of pohutukawa with a picnic table and toilet nearby. It then crosses the dunes, exiting at the northern end of the beach.

In 1993 Jane Campion's Oscar-winning film *The Piano* was shot at Karekare. The beach was cleared of walkers and swept clean during the filming. Karekare subsequently became a popular location for fashion shoots, television commercials and music videos.

# Piha

You can see the wind at Piha in the shape of the rocks, cliffs and offshore stacks. Nun Rock, at the southern end, has a streamlined windward face, while the jagged landward side is a convoluted jumble of rock detritus.

Similarly, the dominant and majestic form of Lion Rock tells a story of the erosive powers of wind, wave and water, which have all contrived to sculpt a bizarre and awe-inspiring rock stack. Lion Rock was known as Te Piha to Te Kawerau a Maki people. They thought the wave patterns at the base resembled those of the bow of a waka. You can climb Lion Rock via a steep track aided with steps most of the way. This gives unparalleled views of the entire tanned and black sands of Piha. The sombre hues of rock are smothered with flax and pohutukawa and only the bright specks of houses are conspicuous from the subtle blend of colours.

Piha is immensely popular with surfers and is internationally recognised as one of the top surfing locations in New Zealand. In the 1930s, Californian lifeguards visited and brought their 9ft-long balsawood Malibu boards. They started a craze, which peaked in the 1970s and firmly entrenched Piha on the international surfing map. Numerous breaks exist all along the beach.

Piha lagoon is a short walk from the beach in front of the campground and is suitable for young children to paddle or row inflatables in. If signs are posted because of bacteria levels, this indicates a lack of recent rain to flush the settled water.

The beach is notorious for rips and holes and is very dangerous for swimming. Two Surf Life Saving Clubs patrol the beach, with the Piha Surf Life Saving Club at the southern end and the United Surf Club at the northern end. Piha Surf Life Saving Club was founded in 1934 and is recognised as one of the best in the country. It needs to be, given the number of rescues it has to perform, especially during the busy summer months.

In late autumn the International World Oceanman event takes place around Piha. This high budget, high profile international event focuses millions of television viewers' eyes on Piha. Numerous television advertisements have also been shot at Piha and the location is popular with film crews for its dramatic scenery and wild atmosphere.

The Piha Stream splits the beach in two. North, Seaview Road turns into Marine Parade North at the beach and continues behind the dunes where there are parking areas and toilets. The road veers inland around Marawhara Stream and Wekatahi Creek and rejoins the beach at the United Surf Club. There is parking and toilets by Les Waygood Park. The road continues to a large parking area at the northern end of the beach.

The southern portion of the beach is accessed by turning left into Beach Valley Road before crossing the bridge over Piha Stream. The road forks shortly after; right leads to a parking area with a takeaway, left heads to another parking area. A toilet block is centrally located between the two.

Walks depart from both ends of Piha Beach. At the southern end the Tasman Lookout Track is signposted and takes 15 minutes along a well-formed and even track to The Gap. This break in the rocks by Taitomo Island is a spectacular display of foaming water, especially in large swells.

At the northern end, the Laird Thompson Track is signposted. This links with the Rose Track and takes 45 minutes to reach White's Beach. The steep walk is worthwhile for views down the beach and the relative seclusion of White's Beach. This was named after John White, a keen ethnographer with a passionate interest in Maori culture. He negotiated the initial sale of land from Maori. There is a deep-sea cave at the northern end of the pristine beach, with mussels and barnacles encrusting the rocky conglomerate. Ramshorn shells abound.

Piha is a nesting area for the blue penguin, which inhabit the caves and rocky areas at both ends of the beach and around Lion Rock. Pied shag and spotless crake are other notable birds of the area.

Fishing from any of the rock shelves under the headlands is good, but you should be especially wary of rogue waves and treacherous surf conditions. Check tides and seek local advice before venturing on to the rocks. Dawson's ledge near The Gap is a popular and dangerous spot, named after Mr Dawson, who escaped a near-drowning in 1900.

Between 1910 and 1921 a sawmill was established to process the numerous kauri logs brought down from the inland ranges. A tramline was built, which was constantly in need of repair from stormy seas and encroaching sands. A few trestle stumps are sometimes visible poking above the sand at Wekatahi Creek.

Piha is accessed along Piha Road from Waiatarua. It has a campground, store and takeaway, but no motels. Private accommodation is also available. Expect the beach to be especially busy during the summer holidays.

## Bethells Beach/Te Henga

There is a subtle contrast of colour in the landscape around Bethells Beach. The sombre hues of the angular cliffs are tinted green with flax and manuka, while the black sands are diluted with a tanned brown. Marram and pingao cap the tops of the extensive dunes, which reach back to the parking area.

Bethells Beach lies at the mouth of the Waitakere River and was formerly known as Waitakere Beach. A floodplain of raupo, flax and manuka spreads to the open, exposed beach, and is bounded by high hills on all sides.

It is a five-minute walk on firm sand alongside the river to reach the beach. You can head left and walk in front of the dunes, and at mid-low tide cross the rocky outcrop before the southern limit and explore the hemispherical sea cave at the base of the cliff.

The European name of the beach is derived from Francis and Mary Bethell and their seven children, who arrived from Wales in 1858. John Bethell was their best-known child, who remained in the area and was fondly known as 'Pa Bethell' until his death in 1942.

Although the current often runs swiftly at the mouth of the Waitakere River, it is usually narrow and shallow. At high tide the crossing may be more difficult and the high water also encloses the spectacular pohutukawa-covered Ihumoana Island.

Cross the small beach framed with cliffs, and climb the low dunes at the base of Erangi Point. This was named after a courageous Maori woman who swam 3 km to Puketotara, with a baby on her back, to meet her lover. You come out above O'Neill Bay. This is a popular place for surfers, with waves forming around Kauwahaia Island. In smaller swells, Bethells also has good waves behind Ihumoana Island and surfable beach breaks. O'Neills Bay was formerly known as Kauwahaia. In the centre of the bay is a rock pinnacle called Tikinui, where a Maori chief named Taratuwhenua speared a young man who was engaged in a clandestine love affair with his daughter.

Artists and photographers are drawn to the beauty and inspiration of Bethells Beach. It has been the setting for the popular television series *Hercules: The Legendary Journeys* and *Xena: Warrior Princess*.

The parking area has toilets and a nearby store and café operate over the summer. There is a Surf Life Saving Club but, as always, you should be very wary of swimming on the west coast. Rips, holes and undertows are common and become stronger in bigger swells. By the carpark the creek is shallow and suitable for toddlers to splash in.

Bethells Beach is accessed via Bethells Road from Waitakere.

## Muriwai Beach

The main attractions of Muriwai Beach are concentrated at its southern end, on and around Otakamiro Point. From any of the vantage points on the headland you can gaze northwards towards the gentle curl of sand, which dissolves nearly 50 km away to a salt-laden haze and the end point of the beach at Kaipara South Head.

Sand blown by prevailing southwesterly winds has formed the characteristic straight profile of the peninsulas north of the Auckland isthmus, with the former coastal indentations now sheltered by the Manukau, Kaipara and Hokianga harbours.

Muriwai is a sand highway and designated road. In 1918 a local farmer, William Jones, was the first person to drive on the beach. He was pulled out by horses when he got stuck. In March 1921 the first motor race was held. William Hamilton, later inventor of the jetboat, broke the 100mph record and took three miles for his acceleration run. His feat was performed in front of a crowd of 6000.

Muriwai Regional Park occupies the land bordering the black sands and is well furnished with facilities.

Turn right from Motutara Road before the carpark at the road-end to access the campground. There is further parking, toilets and picnic tables on the same access road. It is a short walk over the dunes to the beach. A shaded footpath leads south past the Surf Life Saving Club to the main parking area, where there are also toilets and barbecues. A takeaway, small shop and parking area are situated nearby.

Muriwai is one of New Zealand's most dangerous beaches. Only swim when the beach is patrolled and always swim between the flags. If lifeguards are not on duty, common sense should tell you to stay out of the water.

Departing from the southern end of the beach is a boardwalk, which climbs to Otakamiro Point and two lookout platforms. These not only provide magnificent panoramas of the rugged coast, but allow close viewing of the gannet colony.

The Takapu Refuge was established in 1979 to protect the expanding breeding population of the Australasian gannets, which nested on Oaia Island, 1.6 km offshore. With increased numbers, the gannets have displaced the white-fronted terns from Motutara (which means 'island of terns') Island and formed their distinctive mounded nests atop the spectacular rock stack.

Between July and January, you can observe the gannets as they return to their original breeding grounds, establish partnerships, breed, nest and rear their chicks. The close proximity of the viewing platforms allows you to observe courtship displays, aggressive territorial squabbles (where beaks are locked amid much wing-flapping) and rearing of nestlings. The updraught from the cliffs is also harnessed by the birds to aid take-off. You can watch them swoop and glide before deftly alighting on the hummocky terrain of their nesting grounds.

The tracks over Otakamiro Point are wide and even, with the main gradient occurring on the northern side of the headland. Access for viewing the gannets, which cuts out the sections of gradient, is from the carpark above Maori Bay. This small bay to the south of the point is accessed by turning left into Waitea Road from Motutara Road. Follow signs to the gannet colony. A steep track drops to Maori Bay with its dramatic sheer cliffs.

Interesting rock formations in the cliffs give clues to their geological past. The radiating spikes of angular rock are known as pillow lava and were formed during the undersea eruption of molten rock. On contact with cold water, the outer skin of a lava bubble cools, whilst the enclosed molten rock continues to flow under pressure. It penetrates a weakness in the shell of rock encasing it and explodes like a water-filled balloon, forming a pillow shape. The examples of the differing-sized pillows preserved in the cliffs above Maori Bay are world-renowned.

On the beach, black mussels encrust dark rocks on the sombre black sands. The wind-sculpted rock stacks and reefs of Otakamiro Point rise abruptly, while Oaia Island sits humbly out to sea.

The flat rock shelves at the southern end of Muriwai are among the most dramatic and dangerous places to fish in New Zealand. Rogue waves, the incoming tide and strong winds mean you should be wary of venturing here.

The Australasian gannets at the Takapu Refuge are a short walk from the southern end of Muriwai Beach.

Muriwai Beach and Maori Bay are popular with surfers, especially on an incoming tide. Around the headlands and near the mouth of Okiritoto Stream, approximately 2.5 km north, are the best spots. For 4WD access at Okiritoto Stream, turn right into Coast Road and follow it 1.5 km past the golf course. There is also a large parking area under pine trees for horse floats. The extensive dune-flanked sands are a favourite among horse-riders for a scenic trek.

In 1821 Reverend John Butler, local missionaries and Samuel Marsden journeyed to Kaipara North Head during the summer. Subsequent holiday-makers nearly a century later camped near the beach and guesthouses were available from the early 1900s. Muriwai is still popular today.

If you prefer quiet beaches, Muriwai is best avoided during the long summer holiday weekends. However, if you venture north of Otakamiro Point there is plenty of space on the wide shelf of exposed firm sand, suitable for beach games and blokarting.

Muriwai Beach was traditionally known as 'Te One Rangatira', which means 'the chiefly beach'. Many whale strandings on the beach are recorded, including one that resulted in the death of 72 sperm whales in 1974.

Muriwai is 43 km from Auckland and is signposted from Kumeu.

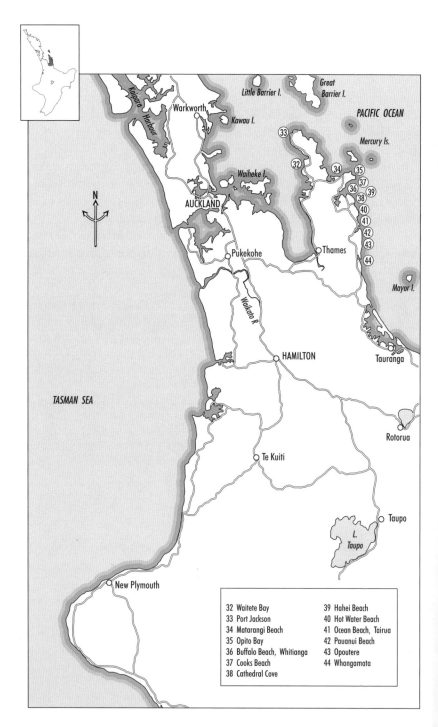

| | |
|---|---|
| 32 Waitete Bay | 39 Hahei Beach |
| 33 Port Jackson | 40 Hot Water Beach |
| 34 Matarangi Beach | 41 Ocean Beach, Tairua |
| 35 Opito Bay | 42 Pauanui Beach |
| 36 Buffalo Beach, Whitianga | 43 Opoutere |
| 37 Cooks Beach | 44 Whangamata |
| 38 Cathedral Cove | |

# Coromandel

For its small area, the Coromandel boasts more than its fair share of beaches. The western side of the peninsula borders the Hauraki Gulf and the eastern coastline is open to the full force of the Pacific Ocean.

An inactive fault line runs roughly parallel with the western side of the peninsula, causing the hills to tumble steeply to the rocky shores of the Hauraki Gulf. The coast is relatively sheltered and is less prone to the erosive power of the waves. Consequently there are few sandy beaches on this side of the peninsula, except Waitete Bay north of Coromandel township.

In contrast, the eastern shores are brimming with golden sandy beaches, enclosed by forest-covered headlands. Drowned river valleys with extensive estuaries and long sandspits form more beaches. Some towns, such as Whitianga and Pauanui, are well developed and have been popular summer holiday destinations for decades. Others have been more recently discovered or are too remote for substantial subdivisions.

Most beaches face east and are ringed by pohutukawa. Surfing is popular all along the coast, especially in easterly swells. Destinations such as Whangamata and Hot Water Beach are among the most frequented surf destinations in the country. Hot Water Beach is also the place to dig your own spa in the sand.

During the summer months the well-known beaches can be very crowded, but you are never far from another more peaceful gem.

## Waitete Bay

The majority of the Coromandel Peninsula's west coast is characterised by steep hills tumbling straight to the colourful waters of the Hauraki Gulf. Waitete Bay is a rare break in the otherwise rocky coastline. The bay contains some fascinating clues to the geological history of this area, which are evident if you know where to look.

At the southern end of the beach, two layers stand out in the rock strata. The bottom layer is ancient greywacke, which was formed around 140 million years ago. The strata of sandstone and mudstone, which were originally horizontal, have since been wrenched by the earth's crustal movements to lie at a steeply inclined angle. Their passage upwards is abruptly halted by a layer of conglomerate, which is composed of sandstone, limestone and other rock detritus. This was laid down 25 million years ago.

This juncture between two layers of rock laid down non-consecutively is known as an unconformity. In this case the time gap between the greywacke and conglomerate is 115 million years.

The conglomerate was later overlain by sand, which was deposited in a coastal environment similar to the conditions prevailing today. Occasional rocks at the foot of the bank above the beach contain the fossilised shells of oysters, which inhabited the shallow marine environment 25 million years ago. They were trapped in the rock as the sand turned to sandstone. The species of giant oyster is now extinct, and was known to have grown rapidly and lived in shallow waters. The layers of shell are clearly visible, and in some specimens you can visualise the oyster's anatomy.

Waitete Bay is a secluded haven of golden sand, with steep headlands enclosing it at either end. The extensive rocky coastline nearby offers a choice of fishing spots with views over the Hauraki Gulf. The calm waters are sheltered and generally safe for swimming, snorkelling and diving. The beach is 300 metres long and covered in golden sand. At high tide the usable beach area can be limited.

Waitete Bay is 18 km north of Coromandel township. Turn left into Waitete Bay Road at the hairpin bend just after Amodeo Bay. You will have to park on the roadside and scramble down a steep bank to access the beach.

## Port Jackson

Curving gently around the Coromandel's northernmost bay, the beach at Port Jackson is a fitting finale to a drive along the peninsula's west coast. From north of Colville, the unsealed road skirts the coastline, passing under 150-year-old pohutukawa, whose gnarled branches reach lazily for the pebbles on the rocky foreshore. Rusting farm sheds, dilapidated cottages and the occasional gate across the road are the only signs of civilisation.

On climbing inland, the precipitous road reaches a lookout far above Port Jackson. There are views north across the Colville Channel to Great Barrier Island and west over the Hauraki Gulf to Waiheke Island and

Greater Auckland. On a clear day you can even see Bream Head near Whangarei. During World War Two, a naval base was built on the hill above the bay to survey the Hauraki Gulf. The building was later used to construct the Colville Store.

Port Jackson was the site of fierce Maori battles in 1828 between Ngapuhi and Ngati Maru. For many years afterwards the area was declared tapu (sacred). Maori were attracted to the area by the abundance of snapper, kingfish and hapuku. The fishing is still good from the rocky headlands either side of the beach.

You can take a walk to the site of an old whaling station that was formerly in operation near Cape Colville, the most northerly point on the Coromandel Peninsula. Little remains except evidence of the tram rails.

On the opposite side of the bay are the remains of an old jetty, which was used in the early 1900s to load barges with flax. Barges were packed at low tide when they were stranded on the seabed and floated away fully laden on the high tide.

Port Jackson is a gently shelving beach with a wide strip of firm flat sand exposed at low tide. It offers safe swimming and is a family beach, suitable for beach games. A DoC campground with piped water, showers and toilets runs the entire length of the beach. The nearest shop is at Colville, 30 km away. As the area is a farm park, dogs are not allowed.

The gentle arc of Port Jackson is a highlight of the scenic drive up the Coromandel's west coast.

## Matarangi

Matarangi is a 5 km-long sandspit that separates the Pacific Ocean from Whangapoua Estuary. The immaculate stretch of sand faces northeast with expansive views of Great Barrier Island and the Mercury Islands.

The waters of the Whangapoua Estuary are filled with stunted mangroves and salt marshes. The skyline behind is dominated by Castle Rock, a volcanic neck which resembles the form of a sleeping giant.

The main access to the beach is via Ocean Road, which is reached by turning left at the roundabout on Kowhai Crescent. The beach is wide and suitable for beach games. Boogie-boarding in the surf and swimming in calm conditions are generally safe. Windsurfers are attracted to the area in easterly conditions and also to the sheltered waters of the Whangapoua Estuary.

Behind the beach, in an almost unbroken strip, is a grass reserve which divides the beach from the mass of holiday homes that now cover the sandspit.

Take a walk to the northern point, where oystercatchers and terns guard the confused waters at the mouth of the estuary. You can glimpse some of the most expensive holiday homes in the country through the pines.

You can launch boats at the southern end of the beach. Just before leaving Matarangi turn left into Kenwood Drive and then right into Goldfield Drive. This veers left into Bluff Road and the access point is just to the left. There are picnic tables on the grass reserve.

You can also follow Bluff Road from the turn-off at the northern end of Kuaotunu, 2 km from the Kuaotunu Store. This spectacular, single-lane, unsealed road perches on the edge of the hillside, with a treacherous drop to the hidden coves below.

Matarangi has a general store, golf course and holiday homes for hire. It is situated 26 km north of Whitianga and signposted from SH25.

## Opito Bay

Nestled on the eastern fringes of the Kuaotunu Peninsula, Opito Bay is a sweeping expanse of golden sand. The wide beach and generally gentle surf make Opito ideal for family fun.

The southern headland was formerly a pa site. Ngati Hei have mana whenua (local authority) and the area has been settled for over 700 years. A 15-minute one-way track leads to the top of the headland, which hides some spectacular cliffs and coves on its southern side. The track can be steep in places, but there are steps to help you. The view of the beach's perfect arc of sand with its white border of broken waves is ample reward for your climb. The Mercury Islands and numerous other offshore islands shimmer in the haze.

Tahanga Hill dominates the beach at the southern end. It is composed of fine-grained basalt rock, which the early Polynesian settlers used to carve adzes. Archaeological evidence has uncovered them as far north as Houhora and south to Taranaki.

Boat-launching facilities are situated towards the southern end of the beach, where there are also public toilets. More toilets are situated near Stewarts Stream. Picnic tables are dotted all along the beach. There is a grass reserve at the southern end of Opito Bay Road.

Opito Bay is 8.5 km from Kuaotunu along the unsealed, winding and steep Black Jack Road. There are a few holiday homes for rent and the nearest shop is at Kuaotunu.

## Buffalo Beach, Whitianga

The broad sweep of Whitianga's Buffalo Beach is best enjoyed near the mouth of the estuary. The small passenger ferry shuttling between the town and Ferry Landing on the opposite shore lends a bygone charm to the river mouth.

You can while away time at the end of the day watching the returning fishing boats unload their bounty on the wharf. Troops of children often fish from the wharf, while parents bait the hooks and applaud the successful catches.

Teams of pipi collectors crouch over the bar at low tide and are joined by fishermen exploiting the twice-daily flow of nutrients washed over the beds. Throngs of variable oystercatchers and red-billed gulls argue over the detritus and boisterous black-backed gulls bully them all. While walking over this end of the beach, there is an unnerving crunch as discarded shells break under your feet.

A row of phoenix palms planted in the 1930s lends a tropical feel to the Esplanade. Enterprising pohutukawa have exploited clefts in their trunks and sprout their branches from the trees' base. Benches beneath the palms are good places to eat ice-creams and fish and chips.

A rock wall occupies the central portion of the beach and arrests the erosive power of the waves during northeasterly storms. It is only possible to walk continuously along the beach at mid-low tide. During storms or spring tides the easterly swell can pound the defences that protect Buffalo Beach Road.

Further up the beach there are toilets opposite Halligan Road. Near the mouth of Mother Brown's Creek, barbecues (coin operated) and picnic tables are provided.

The northern end of the beach is known as Brophy's Beach. The water here is shallower and the beach more sheltered. The grass reserve and children's playground behind the beach make this area suitable for young families. Windsurfers often use the large grass reserve for setting up their gear. Kayakers also launch craft from here and can explore the sheltered waters of Mercury Bay and the mangrove-filled Whitianga Estuary. Ski lanes are situated at Brophy's Beach and near the wharf.

Buffalo Beach is generally sheltered and safe for swimming, with the best surf for boogie-boarding in the central portion by the small carpark and toilets. The beach takes its name from HMS *Buffalo*, a convict ship that sank off the northern headland in 1840. In later storms, leg-irons and shackles were found washed up at Brophy's Beach.

Following the immense 1960 earthquake in Chile, people on the east coast of New Zealand, including Whitianga, became very worried about the possible effects of the ensuing tsunami. After a few days of tension, the wave arrived. Rather than swamp the town as had been feared, the tidal wave merely broke the moorings of vulnerable boats and altered the frequency and amplitude of the tides.

One side effect of the abnormally low tides was the exposure of the remains of HMS *Buffalo*. Some enterprising residents took advantage of the circumstances and set about trying to salvage the wreck. They were thwarted by the rapid flow of the tides and only managed to pull a few timbers from the hull. The anchor from the ship and a commemorative plaque in memory of the sailors who lost their lives in the wreck are displayed around 500 metres from the wharf behind the beach.

## Cooks Beach

Cooks Beach is steeped in history, mostly related to the visit of Captain Cook in November 1769. HMS *Endeavour* dropped anchor on 3 November near the eastern end of the beach. After some wary initial interactions with local Maori, Cook's landing party came ashore and began trading.

In exchange for potatoes, nails and cloth, the crew of *Endeavour* received a selection of fish, which Cook noted were as tasty as he'd ever eaten. He was also impressed with the abundance of shellfish, including cockles, clams and mussels. He renamed the Purangi River 'Oyster River' on account of the delicious oysters he tasted.

The Purangi Reserve accesses the lower reaches of the Purangi River. The water here is shallow, sheltered and ideal for young children to play in. This is a tranquil place to enjoy a picnic and there are toilets, a boat ramp and a children's play area nearby.

On 9 November, Captain Cook and Charles Green, the ship's astronomer, came ashore to observe the transit of Mercury across the face of the Sun. By accurately recording the Sun's altitude and the time the passage took place, they were able to calculate their latitude and longitude. Mercury Bay thus received its European name and positioned New Zealand in relation to the rest of the known world.

Cook noted that the patterns in the rocky headland at the western end of the beach resembled the face of an orator. He thus named it Shakespeare Cliff. There is a 30-minute walk, which climbs the headland from the western end of Cooks Beach. The track passes Lonely Bay, an appropriately named cove which basks in splendid isolation. The lookout point at the head of Shakespeare Cliff affords magnificent views of Cooks Beach, Lonely Bay and Mercury Bay. Two plaques commemorate Cook's visit.

Before leaving the bay, Cook climbed a low hill on the far side of the Purangi River and placed the Union Jack. This action claimed New Zealand for His Majesty George III and Great Britain.

The beach is gently shelving and generally safe for swimming. It is 2 km long and faces north. At the western end near the mouth of the Purangi River there is a significant bar which is often visited by shellfish collectors.

The main access to the beach is along Banks Street near the shops. Turn right into Captain Cook Road on entering the settlement. There is a campground and other accommodation at Cooks Beach.

# Cathedral Cove

The rock arch at Cathedral Cove forms a magnificent entrance hall to the beach. The sounds of crashing waves, the voices of excited children and exclamations of wonder echo through the natural cavern.

Framed by the triangular outline of the cavern entrance, Te Hoho Rock stands majestically at the northern end of Cathedral Cove. Sheer cliffs tumble to the rear of the beach and are fringed by a necklace of impossibly perched pohutukawa. The sand is derived from the ivory-coloured ignimbrite rock and is tinged pink from finely ground scallop shells. The pale shade of the sand dilutes the water colour, so in fine weather it radiates a strong turquoise and resembles a tropical lagoon. The beach is perfectly relaxing, secluded and generally safe for swimming.

Much of the rock in the region was ejected by a fierce volcanic eruption around 8 million years ago. This loosely bound matrix of ash and pumice has been eroded by rain and wind to form a weathering pattern resembling honeycomb. You can see the lattice pattern on Te Hoho Rock and the headlands.

Cathedral Cove is reached by a 45-minute one-way walk. Follow Grange Road up the steep hill from the shops in Hahei. The start of the walk is signposted from the carpark, with nearby toilets. The even and metalled surface has some inclines with short detours to Gemstone Bay and Stingray Bay. The track drops to Mares Leg Cove, where more toilets are hidden in the trees. The cove is named after an unusual rock formation which resembled the hind leg of a mare and collapsed in the 1970s. From here you walk through the majestic entrance to Cathedral Cove. You should carry water, as the walk can be hot in summer.

This stretch of coastline forms part of the Te-Whanganui-a-Hei Marine Reserve, which was gazetted in 1993. It covers 9 sq km and protects the marine landscapes and all life within them. The site was selected on account of its rich and varied marine habitats, which include extensive reef systems, *Eklonia* forests and sponge gardens. DoC provides a snorkel trail at Gemstone Bay, with underwater plaques explaining the marine features. The colourful coastline is worthy of underwater exploration.

The many offshore islands are sacred to the local Maori, who arrived here in around AD 1350. On sighting Motueka Island, the shipmaster Hei proclaimed ownership of the area by referring to the shape of the island as resembling the outward curve of his nose. The spectacular headlands that weave along the coastline formed pa sites, one of which is bisected by the sea cave at the entrance to Cathedral Cove.

The curious rock arch was formed by the erosion of a weak portion of the rock, chiselled by the relentless pounding of the waves. These enlarged an opening, which eventually met its partner on the opposite side of the headland.

Te Hoho Rock, which towers 30 metres above the sea, is an offshore stack and the final stage in the process of coastal erosion. Such stacks are formed when the roof of a rock arch or sea cave collapses, stranding a solitary column of rock. The present sculpture perches on a pedestal, carved by the undercutting power of the waves. It will eventually collapse to form a reef.

## Hahei Beach

The ivory sands of Hahei Beach often radiate brilliantly under clear skies and complement the turquoise-blue water. Offshore, the forest-covered islands are scattered liberally and enhance the views north to the Mercury Islands.

The surf is generally safe and the waves break evenly. The wide beach allows for plenty of games, but during the summer months space can be at a premium. From the northern end of the beach you can follow the signposted metalled track for 30 minutes to the lookout carpark and start of the Cathedral Cove walk.

The southern end of the beach has wooden steps you can climb to join up with the Te Pare Historic Reserve Walk. This 30-minute-return metalled track climbs the headland and affords spectacular views of the waves

Hahei is a popular strip of golden sand on the Coromandel's east coast.

crashing into the offshore islands and reefs. These islands were all named by the sailmaster Hei, who claimed the region for himself and Ngati Hei. With your kayak, you can explore the caves, headlands and jagged seaward cliffs of the islands.

The nearby Te-Whanganui-a-Hei Marine Reserve is a place for fish populations to restock. Fishing off the northwestern headland is prohibited.

The Wigmore Stream at the southern end is suitable for young children to splash around in. The town has shops, accommodation and a motor camp. Hahei Beach faces northeast and is 1.5 km long.

The main access is along Hahei Beach Road, where there are also public toilets and a picnic area. There is also beach access from Wigmore Crescent. Turn left into Pa Road before the settlement and turn left into Wigmore Crescent.

## Hot Water Beach

By a peculiar freak of nature, hot springs have emerged right on the sand at Hot Water Beach. The thermal area is exposed two hours either side of low tide. Armed with a spade you can excavate a private hot pool to suit your requirements. It's a good idea to sink your feet into the sand before digging, as even over a small distance the water temperature can vary considerably. The maximum water temperature is a sizzling 64°C. To turn on the cold tap you will need to find an area where cold water can seep into your pool and balance the temperature. Once you've put in the hard graft, sit back with a cold drink and melt into your handiwork while the kids fortify the barricades against the breakers.

If you don't have a spade, most accommodation in the region can provide one. Alternatively, you can always loiter and pounce on a pool vacated by shrivelled bathers who have finished their spa. If there is an easterly swell, the waves may break too far up the beach for the thermal area to be exposed, so check the weather forecast and seek local advice to avoid a wasted trip. Spas can be invigorating when it's raining. Under a moonlit sky on a warm summer's evening, they are unsurpassable.

Hot Water Beach is popular with surfers, being exposed to easterly swells and the open ocean. There are dangerous rips, so heed the warning signs concerning safe swimming areas. The beach has a Surf Life Saving Club.

The northern reaches of the beach are fringed by dunes and are much less crowded than the thermal areas, which during peak holiday periods are standing room only. Century plants and steep marram-covered dunes border the beach. A small rock-strewn creek empties into the sea. This part of the beach seems a million miles away from the touristy thermal area nearby.

The middle portion of the beach is accessed via an unsealed road, which dives into a parking area with toilets and picnic facilities, 1.7 km from the turn-off to Hot Water Beach Road.

The main parking area at Hot Water Beach has a shop and nearby motor camp. Other accommodation is nearby. You will need to cross a small creek to access the beach from here. The small lagoon above the stream is a good place for young children to splash about in.

Hot Water Beach is signposted from SH25.

At Hot Water Beach you can dig your own spa right on the beach.

## Ocean Beach, Tairua

Ocean Beach is dominated at its southern end by the majestic twin peaks of Paku Hill. This extinct volcano is a rhyolite dome whose flanks are covered with expensive homes. Take a drive up the hill and see the views that attract the property owners.

You can explore the unusual rock formations at the base of Paku by rock-hopping from the southern end of the beach. On the outer extremity of the promontory at Tokaroa Point is a towering pinnacle of rock waiting to tumble to the sea.

The beach is a 1.5 km-long strip of milky tea-coloured sand. The sand is as soft as velvet and feels soothing between the toes. It is bordered by substantial dunes. Three accessways reach the beach via boardwalks from Ocean Beach Road and Paku Drive.

There is a Surf Life Saving Club near the southern end of the beach. The beach shelves quite steeply and is enjoyed by surfers, mainly on the right-hand break at the base of Paku.

The Aldermen Islands sit out to sea and were named by Captain Cook in November 1769. He likened them to the Court of Aldermen, as the rock stacks resembled individual members of the court.

Paku Hill dominates the southern end of Tairua's Ocean Beach.

Access to Ocean Beach is via Manaia Road from central Tairua, or via Ocean Beach Road from just north of the town. The main parking area is situated at the northern end and has toilets and a picnic area.

Tairua is a thriving resort town with a good selection of shops, restaurants and accommodation.

## Pauanui Beach

Over the past three decades, Pauanui has become a haven for New Zealand's 'elite', and many of the homes along the beachfront reflect the money spent here on exclusive properties. Wealthy Aucklanders and their exuberant offspring holiday here during the summer months, but out of season the beach is much quieter.

The beach is 2.5 km long and forms a golden chain around the ocean side of the sandspit. A wide grass reserve runs the entire length of the beach. The Surf Life Saving Club is located between Prescott Place and Claxton Avenue off Pauanui Boulevard. There are toilets nearby. Pauanui offers ocean and harbour conditions for windsurfing. Surfers enjoy small swells, especially in the summer months.

The sandspit at Pauanui is one of the North Island's most developed resorts.

Three short walks depart from the southern end of the beach.

Oceanview Loop Track is a 15-minute-return walk along a well-formed track. It climbs gently through pohutukawa-dominated coastal forest and is punctuated with occasional benches from which to admire the views.

The walks to Flat Rock and Cave Bay follow the headland along a well-trodden track. For the first ten minutes to Flat Rock, the track is slightly raised from the foreshore and skirts the coastal forest. There is good snorkelling around Flat Rock. For the next ten minutes the track is a strip of pebbles at the top of a rocky bay. Near the head of the bay is a wave-sculpted cavern with a makeshift bench. This cave gives the bay its name.

The walk to Pauanui Trig should not be taken lightly. It takes three hours return and slightly longer if you return via the Cave Bay Track. The trig track is formed, but steep and slippery. The views north from the summit give a comprehensive view of the plan of Pauanui. Paku and Tairua form a majestic backdrop through the veil of salt haze.

The return via Cave Bay Track is less steep, but longer. There is a denser mat of pine needles from the self-seeded pines that have colonised the hillside. The track exits at Cave Bay, from where the track follows the coastline back to the carpark.

Access to the carpark at the southern end of Pauanui Beach is reached by turning left into Pauanui Beach Road at the second roundabout after entering Pauanui. Where Pauanui Beach Road forks after 0.9 km, take the left fork. The parking area has toilets, benches and picnic tables under pohutukawa trees.

At the northern end of the sandspit and Vista Paku, there is a large parking area under the shade of mature pine trees. A small passenger ferry leaves from the wharf to Tairua. Benches and picnic tables are scattered around the reserve and are fine places to take in the majesty of Paku on the opposite side of the estuary mouth. This is the best spot for fishing. The boat ramp is situated in the reserve, but seek local advice on crossing the bar.

A plaque on the beachfront sits beneath the engine block of SS *Wairoa*, a steamship that ran aground near the beach in 1919, while trying to reach Slipper Island to collect a raft of logs.

Pauanui has a central shopping area, an assortment of accommodation and an airstrip.

## Opoutere

The broad expanse of Opoutere's beach is evident from the moment you exit the track from the pine-covered sandspit near its southern end. Its 5 km of pure golden sand is a haven for birds, including the New Zealand dotterel, variable oystercatcher and Caspian tern. All these birds nest in the southern dunes at the mouth of the estuary.

The Wharekawa Harbour Sandspit Wildlife Refuge incorporates both the estuary and the beach. It is an important nesting site for these endangered birds. In spring and summer the New Zealand dotterels lay camouflaged eggs in shallow nests on the shore. Do not enter the roped areas as eggs can easily be trampled on. Dogs are not allowed in the Wildlife Refuge.

At mid-low tide you can follow the footprints of oystercatchers for 50 paces or more until they encircle a bivalve, where previously the bird devoured the contents to leave an empty shell. The same bird may be only a few metres away enjoying the next course of its breakfast.

The gently shelving beach is generally safe for swimming but beware of occasional rips, especially around the entrance to the harbour.

At the northern end of the beach an exposed outcrop of rock is flawlessly encircled by seaweed, mussels and barnacles. This is a great place for picking through rock pools. You can watch stranded starfish creep imperceptibly to

Building sand sculptures and decorating them with shells at Opoutere.

another burrow, leaving behind a perfect imprint. At the northern headland you can watch flocks of Caspian terns dive like kamikaze pilots, feeding on the large schools that congregate there.

Access to Opoutere is along Opoutere Road, 11 km from Hikuai and 11 km from Whangamata. Parking is a further 4.3 km on the right and has toilet facilities. Opoutere has a youth hostel and motor camp.

The beach is a 15-minute walk through the pines and remains blissfully free of encroaching human developments.

## Whangamata

Whangamata has been a popular surfing destination since the 1960s and is *the* hang-out for party-crazed teenagers during the long summer holidays. Entertainment is provided during the peak season around the Surf Life Saving Club, with beach pageants and bands. These diversions do not stop the usual string of drunk and disorderly arrests during New Year celebrations.

The surf at Whangamata is consistent, which contributes to its popularity as a surf destination. During summer, the water is crammed beyond capacity with young surfers competing for the best wave. Boogie-boarding and body-surfing are also common activities. You should exercise caution with the volume of water-users.

The two main breaks are around the northern end of the beach, at the mouth of the harbour and on the northeast-facing section of the beach around the Surf Life Saving Club. Surf culture also pervades the main street, which offers all the services a beachgoer could wish for. Even if the weather is not conducive to enjoying the beach, the town offers plenty of alternative wet-weather activities.

Windsurfers take advantage of all wind directions except southeasterly.

The beach runs for 3 km in the shape of a dog-leg, with Hauturu Island lying just offshore at the kink. Hauturu Island attracts the sand that naturally migrates along the beach and is forming a tombolo or sandspit. At present, a causeway is exposed around low tide, which is usually lined with fishermen.

The nearest beach access to the town is along Hunt Street, by the roundabout entering the town from the north. The accessways at Whangamata are conveniently numbered: one being at the northern end, nine at the surf club and ten onwards to the south.

The Surf Life Saving Club is off Lowe Street and has toilets nearby. From the town centre head south, and at the roundabout turn left into Ocean Road. A grass domain with picnic tables runs behind the beach along Esplanade Drive.

The beach is popular with families, with the southern end being less frequented. Whangamata has a wide choice of accommodation.

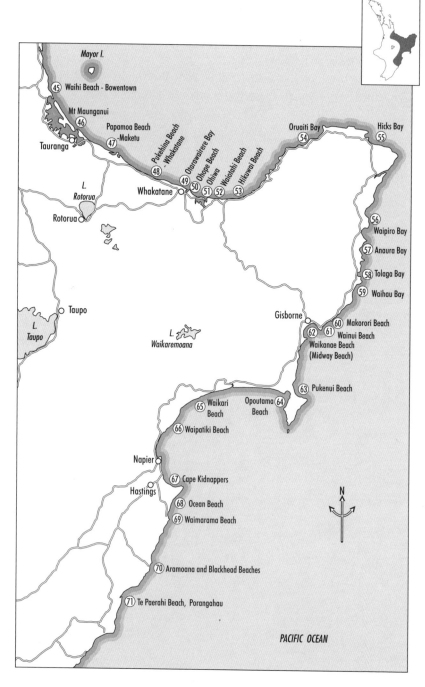

Mayor I.

45 Waihi Beach - Bowentown

Mt Maunganui
46
Papamoa Beach
-Maketu
47
Tauranga

Oruaiti Bay
54

Hicks Bay
55

Pukehina Beach
- Whakatane
48
Otarawairere Bay
Ohope Beach
49
Ohiwa
50
Waiotahi Beach
51 52
Hikuwai Beach
53

L.
Rotorua

Whakatane

Rotorua

56
Waipiro Bay

57 Anaura Bay

58 Tolaga Bay

59 Waihau Bay

Taupo

L.
Taupo

L.
Waikaremoana

Gisborne

60 Makorori Beach

62 61 Wainui Beach
Waikanae Beach
(Midway Beach)

63 Pukenui Beach

65 Waikari
Beach

Opoutama
Beach
64

66 Waipatiki Beach

Napier

67 Cape Kidnappers

Hastings

68 Ocean Beach

69 Waimarama Beach

N

70 Aramoana and Blackhead Beaches

71 Te Paerahi Beach, Porangahau

PACIFIC OCEAN

# Bay of Plenty

The beaches of the Bay of Plenty stretch from Waihi Beach in the northwest to Hikuwai in the southeast. Almost without exception, the beaches are long, flat and rimmed with low-lying land. The expansive stretches of sand cover distances of up to 20 km, broken occasionally by river mouths and estuaries.

The harbours of Tauranga and Ohiwa cover large areas and provide habitat for wading birds, shellfish and other marine life. These bodies of water are protected by beaches such as Mount Maunganui and Ohope on the seaward side of their waters.

Spectacular headlands, such as Mount Maunganui, Bowentown Heads and Te Kohi Point at Whakatane, provide stunning backdrops to the nearby beaches. When explored, they give magnificent panoramas of the beaches.

Most beaches are wide and suited to beach games. Surfcasting is popular and especially fruitful at the river mouths, such as the Rangitaiki River at Thornton. Marine fishing is also popular and there are frequent boat ramps along the coast and up the rivers.

The surf is best in north or northeasterly swells, but the waves are usually smaller than other North Island areas. Mount Maunganui is probably the most popular destination, but breaks exist all along the coast. Sailing is possible for windsurfers in most places and there are plenty of access points to the beaches.

The Bay of Plenty beaches form an arc with White Island at the hub. You can keep note of the wind direction by the plume of steam that usually spews from the vent. The area basks in a mild and stable climate. Most towns offer all the services for a beach holiday. Mount Maunganui is the most developed resort of the region, with high-rise apartment blocks and holiday homes crammed in behind the beach.

State Highway 2 follows the coastline closely, so you are never very far from the beach. In some places the highway is right by the beach, and arching pohutukawa cling to the cliffs above the shore.

Maori have long settled the area and were attracted to the coast by the abundance of shellfish and fish. Pa sites occupied many of the high points both on the coast and inland.

## Waihi Beach to Bowentown

The unbroken stretch of sand from Waihi Beach to Bowentown Heads is the most northern of the Bay of Plenty beaches. It stretches 8 km south in an undulating line to Bowentown Heads at the mouth of Tauranga Harbour. It is a wide beach with golden sand and is generally safe for swimming. It has long been a summer holiday destination and has shops, motels and motor camps.

Waihi Beach is signposted south of Waihi on SH2. Turn right along Seaforth Road to reach Bowentown or turn left for Waihi Beach. Bowentown is also reached from the south by following Athenree Road, signposted from SH2. Athenree Road turns into Steele Road and becomes Emerton Road on reaching the settlement.

At the northern end is Waihi Beach settlement. Near the headland at the road-end is the main access area for the beach, with the Surf Life Saving Club, toilets and picnic tables. Shops and a holiday park are nearby. This end is also the most crowded. The beach runs into a plateau just offshore and is sheltered by the northern headland. Waves lollop gently on the shore in most conditions.

If you dodge the breakers, you can follow a wide and well-formed track for 45 minutes around the headland to Orokawa Bay. This sandy, pohutukawa-fringed beach is untouched by development, save a toilet at the northern end. You can also take a 45-minute-return detour to the William Wright Falls, which cascade 28 metres down a rock face. You will probably get wet feet following the stream to the falls.

South from Waihi Beach there are many other accessways to the beach. In the town, the most notable are from Brighton Reserve (follow Ocean View Road) and Coronation Park. Both have parking and toilets. There are other accessways (indicated by blue posts) if you follow the road closest to the beach. The southern end of Broadway Road has a children's play area and there are toilets opposite the roundabout where Emerton Road reaches Waihi Beach. Surfers visit the beach, especially around the northern headland at Waihi Beach. Windsurfers find the best conditions three hours either side of high tide in a strong southwesterly.

For 4 km to Bowentown, the road runs inland from the dunes. You can access the beach in a few places, but you will need to walk ten minutes across the dunes. The southernmost entry point to the beach is by the motor camp below Bowentown Heads and has toilets. It is signposted to Ocean Beach.

It is well worth spending a few hours exploring Bowentown Heads. The lower carpark at Anzac Bay has toilets and picnic tables. Anzac Bay is ideal for swimming with younger children as it is a sheltered harbour beach.

You can also walk around the headland via a network of walking tracks leading from the lower carpark. Shelly Bay is a ten-minute walk from the carpark. Carry straight on at the intersection of tracks five minutes after the start of the walk. You can also swim here in the more sheltered harbour waters.

From the upper carpark, a track leads to the trig station, which allows magnificent views up Waihi Beach to the north. Southward you can see all the way along Matakana Island to Mount Maunganui and beyond.

The terraces, middens and defensive ditches of Te Kura a Maia Pa are still visible and easily explored. The pa was the site of many battles and its name translates as 'place where young warriors were taught'.

Also from the upper carpark is a five-minute walk down steep steps to secluded Cave Bay. This idyllic stretch of sand is barricaded with huge boulders at the cliff base.

Surfcasting is generally fruitful and the rocky headlands at Waihi Beach and Bowentown Heads are good spots. The boat ramp is situated near the Anzac Bay carpark at Bowentown Heads.

## Mount Maunganui

Mount Maunganui has developed into *the* beach resort of the North Island. High-rise apartment blocks line Marine Parade, which is crammed with shops, cafés and restaurants.

Mount Maunganui Main Beach is a 1 km stretch of fine cream sand, which shelves gently. A northerly swell is popular with surfers. The wide strip of beach above the high-tide mark is perfect for beach games, although during summer it is filled beyond capacity.

Since the 1920s, Mount Maunganui has grown into a popular seaside holiday destination. One of the first Surf Life Saving Clubs in New Zealand was formed here. Even by 1937 Mount Maunganui had a population of 500.

The beach takes its name from Mount Maunganui, a 232-metre, steep-sided dome. This extinct volcano lies in isolation from any other high piece of ground, so not only forms a spectacular backdrop to the beach but commands awe-inspiring views from the summit. You can walk to the top via a network of tracks, which crisscross the steep slopes. Study the information panels at the entrance to the track and allow around 1½ hours for the return trip. All the tracks are wide and well formed but also steep in places.

You can also take a 45-minute-return track around the base which starts from behind the campground and finishes at the top of Pilot Quay. This side of the town faces Tauranga Estuary, the port and city. Pilot Beach is lined with Norfolk Island pines and a grass reserve with numerous picnic tables. Although the beach is more shelly and narrow than Mount Maunganui, its sheltered waters are ideal for young children to swim in.

Mount Maunganui has a wide range of accommodation, and a campground at the base of the Mount has salt-water hot pools. Numerous public toilets, benches and picnic facilities are provided.

The southern end of the ocean beach is hemmed in by Moturiki Island, which is joined to the beach by a causeway. Take a 20-minute-return walk to the end of the headland and gaze back to the beach, town and Mount.

According to Maori legend, Mount Maunganui (Mauao) was one of three hills at the foot of the Kaimai Range. At that time he was nameless and smitten by the beautiful Puwhenua. She was in love with Otanewainuku, a mighty mountain of the region. Because Mauao was nameless, he was rejected. In despair he asked the patupaiarehe (mystical bush fairies) to cast

The beach at Mount Maunganui is the North Island's most developed beach resort.

him to sea. Under the cover of darkness they dragged him to the coast, forming the Waimapu Valley and Te Awanui (Tauranga Harbour). Because the patupaiarehe only work at night, when the first rays of dawn appeared they had to abandon the mountain. Mauao was thus named and means 'trapped by the light'.

After Moturiki Island, Mount Maunganui Main Beach turns into Mount Maunganui Beach and runs several more kilometres. Marine Parade turns into Ocean Beach Road after another 4 km. There are numerous picnic tables and beach accessways across the dunes. Occasional showers and barbecues are situated close to the continuous angle parking along Marine Parade. From Ocean Beach Road onwards a line of houses separates the beach from the road, but accessways are still plentiful. Mount Maunganui Beach is generally less crowded the further you retreat from the Mount.

Boat launching facilities and limited trailer parking are provided at the base of Pilot Quay.

## Papamoa Beach to Maketu

Where Mount Maunganui Beach runs into Papamoa Beach is indecipherable. The unbroken stretch of almond-coloured sand stretches nearly 20 km from Mount Maunganui to Maketu.

The main entrance to Papamoa Beach is from Papamoa Domain. The Domain has a motor camp, parking, toilets and Surf Life Saving Club.

A southwesterly wind with an ocean swell offers the best conditions for windsurfers.

The seemingly endless stretch of sand is gently shelving with a rolling surf. The wide strip of sand above the high-tide mark is suited to beach games or sandcastle building. The beach around Papamoa is often quieter than nearby Mount Maunganui, so is a good location to escape summer crowds. Papamoa has a café, restaurant, shops and boat-launching facilities.

Maketu forms the southern limit of the beach. The mouth of the estuary and the extensive salt marshes behind make reaching the sandspit on the far side of the town difficult and dangerous. This is a New Zealand dotterel breeding ground and should be left undisturbed.

Maketu's accessible beach is limited to a narrow strip of bronze sand on the southern side of the estuary. It's a popular spot for fishing and has a store with a café, motor camp, picnic facilities, toilets and a Surf Life Saving Club.

On the grass reserve behind the beach is a memorial to the Arawa confederation of tribes. Maketu was the landing-place of the *Arawa* canoe and a pa site was situated on the southern headland.

## Pukehina Beach to Whakatane

This sweeping expanse of golden sand stretches over 20 km to form another typical Bay of Plenty beach.

At the very western end of Pukehina Beach is the settlement of Pukehina. You can take a walk to the mouth of the Waihi Estuary and admire the quaint cabins on the opposite shore in Little Waihi, a remnant of bygone times.

The area is known as Dotterel Point on account of the New Zealand dotterels that nest here. Vehicle access is forbidden. A Surf Life Saving Club, toilet and picnic facilities are located nearby. The 4 km stretch of beach at Pukehina has four accessways with parks and children's play areas at each entrance. Pukehina has shops and a takeaway.

Access to Pukehina is also via Rogers Road, which veers left along the beachfront, 4.6 km east of Pukehina along SH2.

Pukehina Beach merges with Kohioawa Beach at Otamarakau. This stretch of coastline has a character of its own. Flanking the road are 30-metre-high

Pack the sausages and an old baking tray for a barbecue on the beach near Whakatane.

cliffs of ivory-coloured volcanic pumice smothered in pohutukawa. Toetoe, manuka and raupo cover the wetlands behind the dunes. State Highway 2 follows the beach and railway line closely.

The first access to Kohioawa Beach comes just after descending the hill into Otamarakau. After a further 5.5 km is Pikowai campground, with toilets and picnic facilities. You will need to cross the railway line.

Kohioawa Beach is wide and steeply shelving, though generally safe for swimming. Its grey sand is overlain by a coarse layer of broken shell, which is crunchy and soothing to walk on. The next access with a parking area is 5.3 km past the campground. Another access with a motor camp is a further 2 km. Fishermen line this stretch of coastline and form part of the scenery.

The next settlement is Matata, which has a campground sandwiched between the beach and Matata Lagoon Wildlife Refuge Reserve. The lagoon is one of the last remnants of coastal freshwater wetlands, which used to be abundant in the area. It forms a home for matata (fernbird), spotless crake, Australasian coots, black teal and little black shags. A white heron also graces the lagoon with its presence from March to October. Whitebait, eels and bullies live in the water. There is also a boat-launching ramp.

After Matata, turn left into Thornton Road, which is separated from the coast by low-lying and swampy paddocks. Some 7.5 km from Matata, the next beach access is along Walker Road, which involves a five-minute walk across the dunes. After a further 3.5 km, Thornton Beach Road leads

Fishing is popular at the mouth of the Rangitaiki River.

to Thornton Beach. There is a boat-launching ramp near the mouth of the Rangitaiki River. The bar can be treacherous around low tide so seek local advice before going to sea. Toilets, picnic tables and a children's play area are nearby.

The course of the Rangitaiki River has been diverted, which led to the area around the river mouth being used as a sand mine. The river has two hydro dams upstream that determine its flow.

To access the Whakatane end of the beach turn off SH30 into Thornton Road, then shortly after turn right into Golf Links Road. Continue straight ahead along the unsealed road after the turn-off to the aerodrome.

Driftwood ejected from the mouth of the Whakatane River is sprinkled along the forefront of the dunes. Kohi Point is visible in the distance. You can even see the beaches of Whale Island (Motuhora), 6 km offshore. This is a wide stretch of beach, sprinkled with flotsam.

There is another access to Whakatane Beach from Keepa Road, just before the Whakatane River crossing and just after the industrial area on Whakatane's outskirts. Follow Ocean View Road to Pacific Parade, from where access is marked.

## Otarawairere Bay

The only way to access Otarawairere Bay is to walk. Three tracks of varying length end up at the hidden cove.

A steep 15-minute one-way track leads from Otarawairere Road, 4 km east of Whakatane. Most of the houses at the top of the track were built in the 1950s for American executives, who needed luxury when they were visiting the paper mill at Kawerau. The area now offers some prime real estate.

A 30-minute one-way track starts from West End Road at the western end of Ohope Beach. The track commands views along Ohope Beach and beyond to Opotiki. You can stop and watch surfers through gaps in the pohutukawa canopy. The track is steep and uneven in places.

From the western end of Otarawairere Bay, the Kohi Point Walkway winds for 2½ hours to Whakatane. This varied walk encompasses panoramic views to White Island and Cape Runaway, shaded coastal forest and significant Maori pa sites. The two pa have well-preserved features and information panels describing how the pa functioned.

Most of the beach is a mixture of exposed grey rocks and coarse sand. You can laze under the shade of pohutukawa or sit on a driftwood log and contemplate the gentle surf. The beach is generally safe for swimming and at mid-low tide you can explore rock pools and play games on the exposed sandy shelf. The rocky promontories make interesting snorkelling and are good to fish from.

The beach is 1 km long and has a toilet.

## Ohope Beach

Ohope Beach is an 11 km-long north-facing sandspit that separates Ohiwa Harbour from the Pacific Ocean. From the lookout on Otarawairere Road, 4 km east of Whakatane, you can clearly see its finger-like form, edged with fine golden sand.

Dropping down the hill from Whakatane, the first access is from West End Road which has a parking area, toilets and picnic tables. The track to Otarawairere Bay leaves from the coastal bush at the far end of the beach. At the junction with Pohutukawa Avenue is a children's play area, toilets and the Surf Life Saving Club.

The long finger-like sandspit at Ohope shelters Ohiwa Harbour.

Driving east along Ohope Beach follow Pohutukawa Avenue, which turns into Ocean Road. There are numerous accessways over the dunes. Toilets are opposite Hoterini Street. Ocean Road ends at Anne Street which turns into Harbour Road. There is no beach access until the Port Ohope Recreation Reserve right at the end of the spit. Dogs are not permitted, as flocks of gulls, terns and oystercatchers feed here at the fertile mouth of the Ohiwa Harbour.

The Ohiwa Harbour covers an area of 2700 hectares and has 86 kilometres of shoreline. Much of the harbour's mud is exposed at low tide, making it a popular place for wading birds to feed. Occasional stunted mangroves anchor in the deep-red silt.

At the Port Ohope Recreation Reserve, a 45-minute return walk crosses toetoe-covered dunes. The piles of driftwood and the extensive estuarine views at the mouth of the Ohiwa Harbour lend a remoteness to the head of Ohope Spit that differs from the bustling holiday atmosphere at the western end.

Ohope Beach is wide and ideally suited to games of petanque, frisbee or cricket. It has safe swimming and a full spectrum of amenities and accommodation. Windsurfers enjoy the forgiving surf breaks and beginners use the calmer water of Ohiwa Harbour. Surfers occupy the break at the western end, in the shadow of the headland east of Kohi Point.

## Ohiwa

Ohiwa's beach is bound at its western end by Ohiwa Harbour. The beach is expansive with a wide strip of sand. It is rarely crowded. Its 5 km of sand is sprinkled with assorted sizes of driftwood over the substantial area behind the high-tide mark. You can collect this wood and build shacks, then decorate them with fallen toetoe stalks and pohutukawa branches. Excavate a hole and barricade it with driftwood to construct a windbreak.

The pa site perched on the pohutukawa-covered cliffs is known as Onekawa. Paragliders often use this hill as a launching point.

To access the western end of Ohiwa follow Ohiwa Harbour Road from 7 km past Kutarere on SH2. There is a motor camp here and you can also launch boats from 1 km inside the Ohiwa Harbour. The bar is sometimes difficult to negotiate.

Ohiwa Spit, at the mouth of the Ohiwa Harbour, is a popular fishing spot and can be accessed by a 15-minute walk from near the campground.

Swimmers need to beware of cross-rips that are sometimes caused here by tidal flow. Captain Cook noted the presence of high dunes at the mouth of the Ohiwa Harbour in 1769. These have since been denuded as the area is prone to fierce dune erosion.

In 1873 a licence was granted for a pub to be opened on Ohiwa Spit, on the condition that the landlord also operated a ferry service to Ohope. This was the catalyst for a small settlement to develop, which included a wharf. Severe erosion always threatened the buildings and by 1915 the area had been evacuated. In the 1960s, further development took place near the spit and chronic erosion continued. In 1978 over 50 metres of foreshore was claimed by the sea, taking many beachfront properties with it.

The warm glow of sunrise on the beach at Ohiwa, near the mouth of Ohiwa Harbour.

Ohiwa Harbour is a quiet backwater, which supports an abundance of shellfish and wading birds. Mangroves reach the southern limit of their world distribution here.

Ohiwa is also known as Bryan's Beach at its eastern end. The settlement of Ohiwa is split between collections of houses at the end of Ohiwa Beach and Ohiwa Harbour roads. Ohiwa Beach Road leads 5 km from SH2, and forks with Ohiwa Harbour Road 1 km from the highway. There are picnic facilities at the end of Ohiwa Beach Road.

Like a scene from a desert island, this shack on the beach at Ohiwa has been constructed from driftwood.

## Waiotahi Beach

Waiotahi Beach extends for 5 km from the mouth of the Waiotahi River to Waioeka River at Opotiki. The western access to Waiotahi Beach is through Waiotahi Domain, which has toilets and picnic facilities. Although the parking area is at the mouth of the Waiotahi River, there is beach access at mid-low tide if you walk 500 metres along the exposed sand from the river mouth to the beach.

The area at the mouth of the Waiotahi River is known as Te Karihi Potae. The naming relates to a legend about Tuamutu, who in order to avenge the death of his father invited Rongopopia to the river mouth for the ceremonial first use of a new net. While Rongopopia's men held the bottom of the line, Tuamutu ordered his men to bring the net over and drown them. The pohutukawa-covered knobs of Tuamotu on the Waiotahi Spit are wahi tapu (burial sites).

The Waiotahi Spit Scenic and Historical Reserve is a further 1 km along SH2 and has picnic areas and a carpark. There are another two access areas, both with barbecues, over the next 1.5 km. There are two carved poles 3 km from the western end of the beach. The carvings depict the history of Opotiki and include the story of two brothers, Tarawa and Tawharanui. They were ancestors of the Whakatohea people, who landed on Waiotahi Beach and released their pet fish, Tanahana, into a nearby spring. The spring later became known as O-potiki-mai-tawhiti, which means 'few pets from afar'. The toilets and Surf Life Saving Club are 200 metres east of the carvings.

Swimming, surfing and sailing are popular all along Waiotahi Beach. This is a good place for beachcombing and searching for interesting pieces of driftwood. The beach faces north and has a wide strip of dry sand. There is a backpackers and campground just before SH2 heads inland. At the eastern end of the beach is the mouth of the Waioeka River, which is a source of the driftwood.

The drive along SH2 passes under pohutukawa, which are anchored to orange cliffs and whose branches touch over the road. This is a spectacular and scenic drive.

## Hikuwai Beach

Heading east from Opotiki, Hikuwai Beach is the last of the expansive Bay of Plenty beaches. This is another sweeping beach, with driftwood scattered over the wide stretch of grey sand above the high-tide mark. The eastern end of the beach is marked by the confluence of the Otara and Waioeka rivers. These large bodies of water drain sizeable catchments inland and transport huge quantities of driftwood expelled during flood conditions.

The first access is 4 km from Opotiki by the roadside and has picnic tables and toilet facilities. The next access is at Tirohanga, where there is a motor camp, store and toilets. You begin to a feel a change in atmosphere heading towards Eastland. Settlements become sparser, the hills near the coast become higher and horses become a more common mode of transport.

Look out for them tied up outside the Tirohanga store. Their riders, often no more than ten years old, are buying lollies in the shop.

Hikuwai Beach turns into Tirohanga Beach at the Tirohanga Stream. There is an unsealed access just before the Tirohanga Store, opposite Tirohanga Road, but there is only limited parking here.

Swimming is generally safe along the beach, and surfing and surfcasting are popular. You can fly kites or play beach games on the soft sand between the driftwood and water mark. Hikuwai Beach is generally less crowded than other Bay of Plenty beaches further west.

The beach 1.7 km from Tirohanga is locally known as Kelly's Beach. Access is unmarked but the beach, which is a two-minute walk over the dunes, has a parking bay.

Some 17.5 km from Opotiki is Opape Road, where there is a motor camp and boat-launching facilities. A gate here may occasionally be closed to vehicle access. At mid-low tide a rocky promontory is exposed below the grey cliffs at Opape. The silhouette of a fisherman seems permanently sculpted into the profile of the rocks. Opape marks the end of the characteristic long beaches of the Bay of Plenty. East from here the beaches become more rocky, isolated and hidden in coves.

# Gisborne and Eastland

Travelling clockwise around SH35 from Opotiki to Gisborne is like visiting a different country. The rugged topography, isolation and sparse population give the district an underdeveloped yet endearing feel. The land is full of surprises, both in the people you meet and the beaches you discover.

From Opape, at the easternmost margin of the Bay of Plenty, the beaches abruptly cease. State Highway 35 climbs steeply over high headlands, providing views to the turquoise water below. Where beaches do occur between the rocky feet of the cliffs, they are composed of smooth pebbles. Vast quantities of driftwood, expelled by mighty rivers such as the Motu, form a gnarled thatch over the bays and coves.

After Te Kaha, the coastal fringe becomes wider and flatter. An abundance of horses graze the verdant green pastures between the road and ocean. Watch for wandering stock and horses on the road. Horses are still a mode of transport, and in places you are likely to see more horse-riders than motor vehicles.

Oruaiti Bay is the only sandy beach on this memorable journey around the northern coastline of East Cape. You are more likely to encounter hoofprints than footprints on the sand. Hicks Bay is the turning point, where SH35 heads inland, passing rusting shacks with satellite dishes on their roofs, endless pasture and pine plantations.

Heading south, the frequency of beaches increases, although they are well-spaced and several kilometres from SH35. There are hidden stretches of golden sand, such as Anaura Bay and Waipiro Bay. Often the beaches are hemmed in by the exposed bluish-grey cliff faces of the characteristic 'papa' rock.

North of Gisborne, the surfing beaches of Wainui and Makorori have long been popular destinations and have nurtured some of New Zealand's finest surfers. Gisborne's Waikanae Beach was the first beach to be sighted by Captain Cook's crew in 1769.

Facilities at some of the more isolated Eastland beaches are limited, so it's best to come prepared to camp. Around Gisborne are all the services holiday-makers require. Most of the Gisborne and Eastland beaches face east and enjoy a mild and sunny climate.

# Oruaiti Bay

Travelling east from Opape and the characteristic sweeping beaches of the Bay of Plenty, SH35 follows the Eastland coast. The road meanders through tiny inlets and coves, then climbs bush-covered headlands commanding panoramic views.

Oruaiti Bay is the first stretch of sand you meet, 94 km from Opape. Its 1.5 km of fine golden sand are sandwiched between the rocky promontories of Waihau Bay and Cape Runaway. The beach faces west and is generally safe for swimming. Steep hills covered in regenerating forest rise sharply from the high and well-developed dunes behind the beach.

Cape Runaway was named by Captain Cook, after he encountered five Maori canoes whose occupants displayed obviously hostile intentions. He ordered one of his men to fire a musket shot, which passed over their heads. They fled in fear, giving Cape Runaway its European name.

You're more likely to see hoofprints than footprints between the pieces of seaweed and driftwood on the beach. This is a great beach to fossick for shards of bone, kina shells and interesting pieces of driftwood.

The main access is mid-way along the beach, and has a shaded picnic area beneath the pohutukawa trees. The parking bay is opposite the motor camp, which also has a store and café.

# Hicks Bay

Hicks Bay is a solitary beach with all the beauty that isolation brings. The beach has two divisions. The main beach is known as Wharekahika, the smaller beach is known as Onepoto. However, there are no accessways to Wharekahika, so it is better to enjoy Onepoto.

After turning into Wharf Road from SH35, turn immediately right and follow Beach Road to Onepoto. Onepoto means 'short beach' but the European name for this idyllic cove is Horseshoe Bay.

This aptly named crescent of deep-tan sand is quaintly proportioned and partially enclosed by a rocky promontory to the north. The southern hills are colonised by kanuka and rise steeply from the foaming water's edge. A 30-minute one-way track leads through this regenerating forest to the motel on the hill. The track is well-formed but steep, and can be muddy. The track starts from the pohutukawa at the southern end of the beach.

The striking form of Nun Rock, Piha Beach.

The towering offshore stack of Te Hoho Rock stands at the northern end of Cathedral Cove.

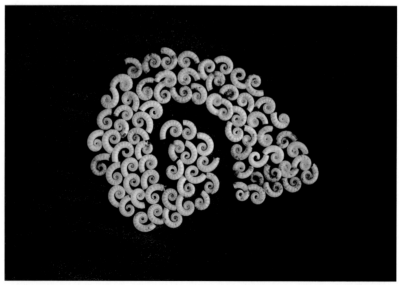

Whites Beach, near Piha, is a frequent setting for environmental sculptures. Make your own.

Karekare is a favourite with beachgoers, artists and film-makers.

Dolphins are frequent visitors to the ivory sands of Maitai Bay.

Orokawa Bay is fringed by a green ribbon of pohutukawa.

Climb the northern headland for spectacular views of the beach at Tolaga Bay.

Wainui is a popular surf beach north of Gisborne.

Raglan is the surfing Mecca of the North Island.

Spirits Bay is the North Island's most northerly beach.

The walk through the disused stock tunnel to Waikawau Beach is like a gateway to another world.

The sand is firm and smooth. The sheltered beach is calm and safe for swimming with young children. The beach is too flat to surfcast; the fishing is better from the rocky promontory or on Wharekahika. Surfers appreciate the waves at the southern point of Onepoto.

There is a toilet at the southern end and parking at the northern end. There is a small settlement at Onepoto with a backpackers.

A store with petrol pumps is located on Wharf Road near the turn-off. Take a drive to the northern end of Wharekahika past the old freezing works. Eventually the road skirts Matakaoa Point and reaches the wharf. This ramshackle, boarded wharf formerly served as a departure point for trams delivering frozen meat from the freezing works to the waiting boats. The works were closed in the 1920s.

Hicks Bay takes its European name from Lieutenant Zachariah Hicks, who was the first crew member aboard the *Endeavour* to sight the bay.

The horseshoe crescent of sand at Onepoto is the best place to enjoy Hicks Bay.

# Waipiro Bay

Waipiro Bay forms an elegant curve, which dwindles to a southern headland with exposed sheer cliffs. Its 4 km of clean sand is unlittered with driftwood. The sandy beach abuts an area of large pebbles at the high-tide mark.

The beach is gently shelving and faces east. It is flanked by narrow dunes, which form the feet of the parched hills above. A sign says swimming up to five days after rain may increase the risk of illness.

There is a parking area below the church with picnic tables, a toilet, and shade provided by the Norfolk Island pines. You can follow the golden sand around the small promontory to view the northern end of the beach. The strip of sand between the high-tide mark and the dunes is only a few metres wide in places, limiting the number of games you can play here.

The area was first settled by the Iritekua whanau (family), a hapu (sub-tribe) of Ngati Porou. The area became a busy port in response to the expanding sheep industry, which developed on the fertile land leased from Maori landowners. In the 1890s, 100,000 sheep per year were shorn in the area. In 1910 the first coach to Gisborne heralded the beginning of motor transport, which started to flourish in the 1920s, bringing about the decline of the port.

R.J. Kerridge started his first picture theatre here in 1923. In 1987 the world premiere of *Ngati* was held in Waipiro Bay. This full-length feature film was shot in the area and used many locals in its cast.

Waipiro Bay's isolation adds to its charm and decreases the chance of seeing too many other people. It's a great spot for relaxing and you are assured solitude outside the summer months.

To access Waipiro Bay from the north, turn left into the unsealed Kopuaroa Road, just after the bridge over the Kopuaroa Number 2 Stream, and follow it for 6 km. From the south, follow Waipiro Road from Te Puia Springs. You may have to travel to Te Puia Springs for shops and services, so come prepared with a picnic.

## Anaura Bay

Anaura Bay is a crescent of fine golden sand which feels like silk to walk on. Its very gentle shelf and sheltered northeasterly aspect make it ideal for swimming in calm conditions. Its 3 km length is enclosed by steep headlands. The pastel colours of the parched grassland and crumbling rock contrast markedly with its turquoise waters. At the southern end, the beach peters out to a rocky bay. The local sea defences here are an example of Kiwi ingenuity and worth an inspection.

The beach is an outstandingly scenic place for surfcasting and the wide beach area makes it perfect for frisbee, cricket or kite flying.

The two-hour-return Anaura Bay walkway departs from near the northern end of the beach. Park by the DoC kiosk just over the bridge. The track crosses private land, so seek local information regarding its condition before attempting it. The walkway traverses native coastal forest, lush streamside vegetation and exotic pine plantations. The views of the bay from the ridge are spectacular. The track is well-formed with marker posts to guide you. Expect to get wet feet in the stream and long grass.

At the southern end of the bay is Motuoroi Island, which was formerly inhabited by Maori, skilled in the working of South Island greenstone.

When Cook arrived on 21 October 1769, he was warmly welcomed by Maori in canoes. He was able to gain supplies of fresh water from the Hawai Stream and recorded the horticultural practices he observed.

Anaura Bay has a DoC campground and motor camp. The main beach access is in front of Anaura Road, close to where it reaches the bay. Anaura Road is 14 km north of Tolaga Bay, where the nearest services are located, and 23 km south of Tokomaru Bay.

The soft sand of Anaura Bay is a joy to feel between your toes.

## Tolaga Bay

Tolaga Bay's beach stretches for 2.5 km in a deep arc, which is separated in the middle by the wide and impassable mouth of the Uawa River.

The sand at the northern end of the beach is the colour of milk chocolate and is sprinkled with driftwood, seaweed and other flotsam. Low marram grass-covered dunes flank the foreshore and a line of Norfolk Island pines borders the road. The gently shelving northern part of the beach is patrolled by a Surf Life Saving Club and is accessed from SH35 via Forster Street. There are toilet facilities at several points along the grass reserve between the dunes and the road.

There is a walk up the cliff face from the carpark at the road-end. Follow the track from the sign at the Tatarahake Cliff – Ernest Reeves Reserve. The steep track is aided by steps. It takes approximately 15 minutes to reach the lookout, with panoramic views over the bay and inland to the pastured hills. The sheer, exposed cliffs stretch out to sea, their bluish-grey 'papa' rock mottled with occasional scraps of vegetation, holding on tentatively in a losing battle with the sea.

Low dunes flank the southern end of the beach. You can take a walk along the 660-metre wharf, reputed to be the longest in the southern hemisphere. It was completed in 1929 and served the busy shipping route on the coast before the construction of the road to Gisborne. It was progressively closed during the 1960s and '70s due to deterioration of the concrete, but today provides a local landmark and a popular fishing spot. A walk along the old

A walk along the crumbling wharf at Tolaga Bay is a highlight of a trip around East Cape.

tramlines on the wharf also gives you a chance to admire the interesting rock formations and strata on the adjacent cliff face.

Tolaga Bay has a motor camp, accommodation and shops.

# Waihau Bay

A small collection of baches is the only sign of civilisation on this otherwise deserted stretch of golden sand. Majestic high headlands stretch into the distance, their exposed walls undercut and given back to the sea. The east-facing beach has a wild and exposed feel, weaving between small spurs and flanked by a narrow strip of dunes that give way to paddocks. Your footprints are likely to be outnumbered by hoof and birdprints.

Bring beach games and a book. This unblemished beach is very relaxing and is suitable to visit as a day trip from Gisborne or Tolaga Bay.

To access Waihau Bay, turn left into Waihau Beach Road. Waihau Beach Road is 13.7 km south of Tolaga Bay. The 6.5 km of unsealed road leads to a grass reserve with toilets. Bring a picnic lunch as the nearest store is at Tolaga Bay. Although the bay stretches to the distant headlands, the usable part of the beach is restricted to a few kilometres north of the parking area.

# Makorori Beach

Makorori Beach is popular with surfers, having a number of different breaks along its length. If you are not a surfer you can sit and watch them, or just boogie-board instead.

The sand is firm but often strewn with seaweed and other debris regurgitated by the sea. The gravel parking area at the southern end is the best place to park, but access to the beach here involves a short but steep scramble down the forefront of the dunes. The only steps are a little further south and involve a walk along the roadside to the carpark. There are occasional grass reserves behind the low dunes.

At the southern end of the beach there is a 20-minute one-way walk, which traverses the headland and provides sweeping views of both Makorori Beach to the north and Wainui Beach to the south. Frequent benches and picnic tables allow you to take in the sounds of the distant surf or watch the harrier hawks circle on the updraught. The walkway starts 500 metres after the road begins to climb at the southern end of Makorori Beach. It finishes in a small gravel parking bay just as you enter Wainui Beach.

The easiest access is at the northern end. Drive up Makorori Beach Road, where there are toilets and picnic facilities. Take a look at the collection of funky old-style beachside houses. Many are painted bright colours, and their gardens are decorated with bizarre sculptures, fabricated from driftwood, bone and rope washed up on the beach.

Wainui has shops and accommodation. Gisborne is 8 km south.

## Wainui Beach

Wainui is a popular beach 5 km east of Gisborne. Its 4 km of golden sand is punctuated by a fenced area planted with coastal trees.

The beach is best enjoyed at the southern end, accessed from Wairere Road. There is a Surf Life Saving Club, children's play area and three accessways with roadside parking. There is also a store, motel and restaurant at this end of the beach. If you follow Wairere Road 1.5 km south, it meets with SH35 again at Oneroa Road. On this section of the beach there are houses between the beach and the road.

The northern end of the beach is separated from the road by high dunes. There are toilets, accessways and picnic facilities near the brightly painted store at Okitu. On 18 March 1970, 59 sperm whales were stranded and buried here. The 47 females and 12 males had a combined total weight of approximately 1800 tonnes. Stop to look at the black-and-white photos on the information panel.

At the northern end of the beach there is a 20-minute one-way walk that traverses the headland. There are sweeping views of both Makorori Beach to the north and Wainui Beach to the south. Frequent benches and picnic tables allow you to take in the sounds of the distant surf or watch the harrier hawks circle on the updraught. The walkway finishes 500 metres before the road drops at the southern end of Makorori Beach. It starts from a small gravel parking bay just before you leave Wainui Beach from the north.

For surfers, the beach is divided into three main breaks and offers good waves on most swells. Windsurfers find the predominant southerly winter winds and northeasterly summer sea breezes the most favourable.

## Waikanae Beach (Midway Beach)

Gisborne's main beach is a long strip of greyish sand that faces south. It is steeped in European history, as this was the first beach in New Zealand sighted by the crew of the *Endeavour*.

At the eastern end, after crossing the Gladstone Road Bridge coming into Gisborne, turn left into Customhouse Street. Where it veers right into Awapuni Street, there is a fine statue of Captain Cook with an information panel describing events concerned with the naming of Poverty Bay.

At the mouth of the channel into the port is a statue of 'Young Nick'. Nicholas Young was the 12-year-old surgeon's son aboard the *Endeavour*. On 7 October 1769, he spied land, receiving a barrel of rum from Captain Cook as a reward. His statue is positioned pointing to Young Nick's Head at the southern end of Poverty Bay. This was the first place in New Zealand to be given a European name.

The mouth of the channel experiences serious rips and cross-currents. It is not suitable for swimming. Fishing is not permitted here, as this is a working passage of water for craft using the port.

Gisborne's Waikanae Beach was the first beach in New Zealand to be sighted by Captain Cook's crew.

Just behind the beach is the Waikanae Cut Reserve, a shaded area under magnolias and Norfolk Island pines. It's a good place on a hot day to picnic and watch the logging ships being loaded from the docks. There is a parking area and a children's play area behind the line of Norfolk Island pines. A ski-lane is also located here. Observe guidelines on the information panel nearby before using this facility.

The next vehicle access west is along Grey Street, near the motor camp and Waikanae Surf Life Saving Club. There is also a store, public toilet and picnic table. West of Grey Street there is a grass reserve lined with picnic tables. The usable strip of beach is narrow, so at high tide you may be limited in the activities you can pursue. Houses line the landward side of the grass reserve.

Heading further west there are accessways along Salisbury Street and Roberts Road. The beach becomes decidedly less crowded here, but the sand is messier with flotsam. Where Salisbury Street turns into Centennial Marine Drive, the Beacon Reserve is immediately on the left. Waikanae Beach merges with Midway Beach here and there is another Surf Life Saving Club with a parking area close by. Changing sheds are situated near the restaurant, with another parking area opposite Stanley Street. Nearby there is an adventure playground with ample parking and picnic areas.

There is another ski-lane opposite Pacific Street with a gravel parking area. Shortly after the old jail there are many grassed parking areas, with beach access across the low dunes.

The road continues past the airfield. There is foot access to the beach, involving a short walk over the dunes, which cross private land. This part of the beach is wilder and more isolated. It leads to the mouth of the Waipaoa River and the rather unsightly road-end. Apart from fishing at the river mouth, there is no need to venture further west than Pacific Street on Midway Beach.

# Hawke's Bay

Although the Hawke Bay coastline around Napier is composed of black shingle, the region of Hawke's Bay hides some attractive and isolated beaches. From the wide beaches of Mahia Peninsula to the secluded gem of Waipatiki, the coastline is studded with attractive golden sandy beaches.

Mahia Peninsula has long been a popular summer holiday destination and offers some fine surf and spectacular scenery. The pastel shades of the parched hills and the atmospheric haze of sea spray lend a timelessness to Mahia. At the southern limit of Hawke Bay (the name given to the bay, not the region) are the dramatic cliffs of Cape Kidnappers and the resident Australasian gannets.

Further south are Ocean Beach and Waimarama Beach, both haunts of Napier and Hastings residents in need of sand and surf. Aramoana and Blackhead Beaches are linked by a stretch of sand and a rock shelf, which is exposed at low tide. These fertile waters form part of the Te Angiangi Marine Reserve and are popular with snorkellers and divers. Te Paerahi Beach at Porongahau is a blokarter's dream, with 16 km of firm, flat sand.

Many of the beaches are off the beaten track and involve a drive over unsealed roads. This shouldn't deter you from visiting, as with isolation often comes beauty.

Hawke's Bay enjoys a sunny and mild climate. Much of the area is devoted to sheep farming. Settlements with services can be sporadic.

## Pukenui Beach (Mahanga Beach)

Oraka Beach forms the most southerly point of Pukenui Beach. From Mahia Beach Store follow New Castle Road for 1.5 km and turn left into Mahia East Coast Road at the crossroads. Just 2 km further on the left is Oraka Beach, where there is a turning area and limited parking.

Although this small area of exposed beach is littered with detritus from the outflow of Maungawhio Lagoon, it makes a great place for shell-collecting. The exposed rock shelf at the southern end is a good local fishing spot. To the north, the distant expanse of Poverty Bay stretches away to a hazy horizon.

To reach Pukenui Beach from Oraka Beach you will need to cross a wide creek. Seek local advice before attempting the crossing, as conditions and depth can vary considerably.

The only other access is from the settlement of Mahanga at the very northern tip of the beach. At the road-end there are toilets and a grass reserve for parking. The beach here is gently shelving and merges with boulders towards the headland. You can look down the entire length of the coffee-coloured sandy beach to the settlement of Mahia.

The low marram-covered dunes merge with the pines at the northern reaches of the beach. Further south, the fertile muds of the Maungawhio Lagoon provide rich feeding grounds for pied stilts and white-faced herons.

Because Mahia Peninsula juts out into the main whale migration route, it became a prominent whaling centre. Around 11 whaling stations were located on the peninsula, one being at Mahanga. Whaling was so prolific that in its heyday one station alone caught 26 sperm whales in a year. By the 1880s there were 450 people, both Maori and European, living off whaling. When stocks became depleted, many ex-whalers pioneered farming in the district and settled here.

Mahanga Beach is 8 km from Opoutama, where the nearest shop and accommodation are located.

## Opoutama Beach

Mahia Peninsula is a craggy appendage of land joined to the mainland by a tombolo, or sandspit. Mahia's two beaches flank this narrow neck of sand, which is the largest tombolo in New Zealand. On the eastern side is Pukenui and on the western side is Opoutama.

Opoutama Beach is an elegant arc of golden sand that sweeps for 5 km around the western side of the tombolo. Its sheltered aspect and gently shelving profile make it a good place for swimming. The southern end is usually more sheltered than the northern end, but this depends on the direction of the swell.

At the northern end is the small settlement of Opoutama, which has a campground and store. Continue past the store and after crossing the railway line turn right into Blue Bay Road. At the road-end there are public toilets and a picnic table.

Heading south, the road is separated from the beach by wide, low dunes. There are only a few poorly formed accessways until you reach the settlement of Mahia Beach at the southern extremity.

Mahia Beach is well furnished with facilities, offering a campground, motel units, café and shop. Boat-launching takes place in the lee of the dramatic headland. The large grass reserve by the potholed parking area has a children's playground, picnic table and public toilets. The beach is better enjoyed at this end. Although the sand is often littered with seaweed, it makes a pleasant place for relaxation and beach games. Surfcasting is popular at Mahia Beach.

Around the headland is a small secluded beach, which shelves gently. There is good fishing off the rock shelf at its northern end. During busy times you can often find peace and solitude here.

Opoutama is 12 km from Nuhaka, and Mahia Beach is a further 9 km.

## Waikari Beach

Access to Waikari Beach is via a 20-minute walk from the carpark at the Waikari Beach Scenic Reserve. Follow the orange markers for five minutes along a well-formed track, which meets with a 4WD farm track. The Waikari River meanders to the left, fanning out to a wide river mouth at the beach.

Waikari Beach is a wild and desolate beach scattered with driftwood logs.

The beach and river meet in a chaotic maelstrom of turbulent water. Driftwood from matchstick size to complete tree trunks adorns the coarse sand. Fine black pebbles congregate in patches where they have been collected by the waves. If you want to find a piece of driftwood to ornament the garden, or polish up for the mantelpiece, then this is the beach.

Dunes barely withstand the wild breakers, and the vertical walls of mudstone behind have an apron of pasture at their bases. Goats browse the grass and add to the wild feeling of the location.

This is an exposed east-facing beach and more suited to exploring and walking than lazing and sunbathing. Its 2 km sweep stretches south towards sheer dramatic cliffs. You can see evidence of a huge landslide, triggered by the 1931 earthquake that flattened Napier and Hastings. It's not safe to venture further south than the end of Waikari Beach, as excessive coastal erosion has made the track unsafe.

To reach Waikari Beach turn into Waikare Road at Putorino, 59 km south of Wairoa and 58 km north of Napier. Follow the unsealed road for 13 km until you reach Waikari Beach Scenic Reserve. This signposted grass area has basic toilets and a picnic area.

## Waipatiki Beach

Waipatiki's short stretch of sand is the colour of the ripe maize prevalent on the nearby agricultural plains. It is composed of a blend of coarse sand and small black pebbles.

At each headland is a precipitous face of stratified mudstone, which abruptly encloses the bay. Goats browse the occasional tufts of precariously growing grass, and pine trees stand atop the hills waiting to fall. Waves crash in bursts of foam on the rocky promontories below. Because of the sheer headlands and steeply rising, forest-covered hills behind, there is a cosy feel about Waipatiki.

Behind the beach is a reserve with toilets and picnic facilities. There is a campground with cabins owned by the local farmer, which looks out on to the beach behind the lagoon. Waipatiki Beach is steeply shelving and generally not suitable for swimming.

Entering Waipatiki, lines of towering kahikatea adorn the roadside and give a clue to the native vegetation that still thrives in the area. This valley exhibits a rare example of intact coastal forest, which used to cover virtually the whole region of Hawke's Bay. A 15-minute one-way walk is signposted from approximately 500 metes behind the beach.

Verdant nikau palms, tall kahikatea and a canopy of tawa are replete with birdcalls and the flapping of kereru wings. Branching from the main track, there is also a 20-minute return walk to a lookout. This track is muddy but well formed and has steps over the steeper ground. There are magnificent views of the beach from the track.

Waipatiki is an isolated and attractive beach, 13 km down the unsealed Waipatiki Road from SH2. Waipatiki Road is 29 km north of Napier. Alternatively follow Tangoio Road (22 km north of Napier) for 6 km, then turn right into Waipatiki Road.

## Cape Kidnappers

Cape Kidnappers takes its European name from an incident that occurred when Captain Cook visited the area in 1769. After trading with local Maori, Cook's Tahitian interpreter Taiota was seized and taken aboard a Maori canoe. He escaped when shots were fired at the retreating waka and managed to swim back to the ship.

The stratified cliffs at Cape Kidnappers have been sculpted into craggy blocks by successive earthquakes.

According to Maori tradition, the Hawke's Bay coastline is the sacred jawbone the mythical hero Maui-Tikitiki-a-Taranga used to fish up the North Island. It is said Cape Kidnappers could be the hook. A walk along the 8 km beach to the cape certainly embodies the legend, as the cliffs protrude majestically, as if thrust up from the ocean.

You can admire the 150-metre-high cliff faces as they rise vertically, displaying bands of multi-coloured rock. Some layers are ivory coloured, originating from volcanic lava flows and ash deposits; some layers are of marine origin, deposited on the edge of a huge continental shelf and metamorphosed to rock containing abundant fossils; other layers are fluvial in origin and are a loose conglomeration of pebbles. The earthy-coloured layers are very clearly delineated and form a mesmerising line that draws your eye along the headland.

Rills have formed grooves down some of the cliff faces, making them resemble giant curtains. Earthquakes have tilted and fragmented the huge blocks to create a sweeping vista along the coastline. It's easy to be captivated by the geological story told in the rocks. At the base of the cliffs aprons of slumped rock are being chipped at relentlessly by waves. A rocky shelf is exposed at mid-low tide to reveal a sandy strip mantled with pebbles.

It's only possible to complete the walk along the beach by departing no earlier than three hours after high tide from Scotsmans Point at Clifton. You need to start the return journey from the cape no later than 1½ hours after low tide. Allow six hours for a return trip, including viewing the gannets. It is unwise to rest directly below the cliffs as small rock-falls may occur. During periods of rain rock-falls may be more frequent.

The Australasian gannet (*Morus serrator*) or takapu uses three sites around the cape for breeding. Up to 6500 pairs breed here, making it the largest and most accessible mainland breeding site of the species in the world.

It is thought gannets started breeding at Cape Kidnappers around 1850. In 1870, Henry Hill, a Hawke's Bay naturalist, recorded 50 birds at the Saddle nesting site. In the 1930s a further nesting site was established on the Plateau (110 metres above sea level). Another site was later started at Black Reef, a collection of rocks reached from the beach before the cape.

The gannetry is empty from May to mid-July, when the gannets return to take possession of the nesting sites. Most eggs are laid in October, making November to February the best time to visit. The site is closed from 1 July until the Wednesday before Labour weekend, to allow for undisturbed courting, nesting and egg-laying.

At the age of four months old young chicks make their astonishing first flight of a massive 2700 km across the Tasman Sea to Australia, where they stay for two to three years before returning to their birthplace to mate.

At the cape there is a picnic shelter and toilets, with an information panel on the geology and the gannets. To reach the plateau colony, climb for 30 minutes up a steep track to a viewing area. From here you can look down on to the saddle colony and the retreating form of the cape. The views of the waves pounding the bluish-grey 'papa' rock stacks and cliffs are spectacular.

Cape Kidnappers is comprehensively signposted from Napier, Hastings and Havelock North. There are no public toilets at the start of the walk in Clifton, but there is a café and motor camp.

The gannet colony at Cape Kidnappers is the largest mainland breeding population in the North Island.

## Ocean Beach

From the roadside before the steep descent to Ocean Beach, there is a lookout which affords views of the entire coastline. The rolling hills, which slope to a wide expanse of reddish dunes, stretch to a misty haze in the distance. Approval has recently been granted for land subdivision, so expect the character of this unchanged piece of Hawke's Bay beach to alter.

Ocean Beach gives you the impression it hasn't changed for a long time. Outside the busy summer period, when visitors flock to its unbroken stretch of golden sand, your only companions on the beach are likely to be white-fronted terns. A collection of classic old-time baches nestles on the far side of the creek.

For 7 km north of the access road, vehicles are permitted on the beach and you can drive all the way to Whakapau Bluff at the northern headland. This was formerly a pa site. A natural rock arch used to lead to the northern coastline, but it collapsed in the 1940s making passage around the headland very difficult.

A whaling station called Rangaiika was situated just north of the Whakapau Bluff from the 1830s. The rusting remains of a few old machines are still visible.

Heading south along the beach past the baches is not possible around high tide. The headland is approximately 2 km distant, and is an interesting place for fossicking in rock pools.

The golden sand is soft to touch, with a wide strip of dry sand suitable for beach games. The beach faces east and is generally suitable for swimming. A Surf Life Saving Club patrols the beach area near the carpark, where there are also public toilets. Three reefs on the beach are used by surfers.

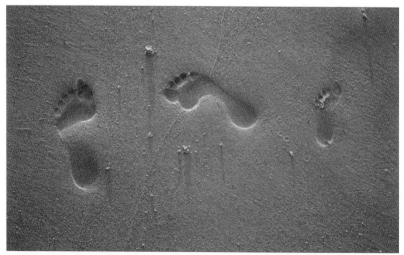

The family's footprints in the sand at sunset.

Because the hill leading to the beach is so steep, it is better to launch your boat from Waimarama Beach to the south.

The entire beach is popular for surfcasting and net fishing. You can find a secluded spot in front of the dunes and admire the changing colour of the water, from denim blue under a cloudy sky to metallic green when the clouds break.

The nearest shops are at Havelock North and there is a campground with cabins 7 km from Ocean Beach.

To reach Ocean Beach from Havelock North, follow Te Mata Road and turn right into Waimarama Road. Ocean Beach is well signposted. After crossing the Tukituki River, turn left into Ocean Beach Road. The last 1.5 km is unsealed except for 400 metres of tarseal, which drops very steeply to the beach. This is a first-gear hill.

## Waimarama Beach

The best access to the beach is from Waimarama Domain, an attractive grassed area behind a bank of native coastal species such as ngaio and taupata, replanted through a community initiative. The domain houses the Surf Life Saving Club, boat-launching facilities, toilets and picnic area. Accessways over boardwalks lead to the pebble fringe. Sand is exposed only after high tide and is generally wet from tidal outflow. If you want a beach to laze and play games on, it is probably better to visit nearby Ocean Beach.

For surfers there are good reef and sand breaks in swells from northeast to south. A southeasterly swell with southwest winds are the favoured conditions. Experienced windsurfers find winds from a southerly direction best. Dangerous rips can develop along this beach and waves break unevenly in places. Seek local advice before swimming.

Sea defences are needed here, as at high tide the waves reach all the way to the forefront of the dunes. Rock walls have been constructed further down the beach to prevent erosion of the beachfront properties.

You can stroll along the beach and look for pebbles to ornament the goldfish bowl or line the flowerbeds. Fishing is popular, but towards the southern reaches the beach becomes impassable except around mid-low tide.

At the southern end you can look out to Bare Island, so named because of the sparsity of vegetation cover. When Cook passed here in 1769, he noticed the island was inhabited. When the French explorer d'Urville passed in 1827, he saw a pa site and named the island 'L'isle sterile' – 'Bare Island'. The Maori name Motukura means 'crayfish island', which indicates the abundance of crayfish in the vicinity.

Archaeological excavations have shown Maori lived in the region from the thirteenth century. When Colenso visited in 1843 he was welcomed by about 80 Maori. Around this time a whaling station was also set up, but no remains are visible today.

Waimarama Beach is 50 km from Napier and 27 km from Havelock North. From the end of Te Mata Road in Havelock North, turn right into Waimarama Road and follow it 25 km to Waimarama Beach. In Waimarama, the domain is signposted from Harper Road.

Waimarama has a motor camp, store and a good number of holiday homes.

## Aramoana and Blackhead Beaches

Aramoana Beach is a perfect semicircle of golden sand. It has a wide usable area in front of the low dunes and is set in a bowl, surrounded by parched grassland. Waves roll in and are funnelled by the curved shape, breaking unevenly along the beach. The area is notorious for rips and holes. At the southern end is a reef that concentrates higher waves. Seek local advice before swimming.

Aramoana is reached by travelling 8 km along unsealed Gibraltar Road, which is on the right just before Pourerere.

Make sure you take a look at the Aramoana homestead on the hill. For obvious reasons, it is known as 'The Castle' and houses the sixth generation of the McHardy family. It was built in 1894 and is a grandiose and stately character homestead. The homestead and woolshed were built of Coromandel kauri. Because of the difficulty of mooring the boats near the shore, the wood intended for construction was thrown overboard and floated ashore on the surf.

Aramoana is connected to Blackhead beach via a 1½-hour return walk along the sandy beach. The walk is possible except around king tides and is best attempted at mid-low tide when the rock shelf is exposed.

The coastal fringe between Aramoana and Blackhead forms the Te Angiangi Marine Reserve. It was established in 1997, covers 146 ha and protects all natural features and marine life in their natural state.

At low tide the broad hammer-marked platform of grey rock is exposed, harbouring a huge diversity of marine life, including kina and paua. The area is at the convergence of the warm East Cape current and the cooler Southland current. The waters thus contain a large variety of species, that feed in the fertile waters.

Blackhead Beach lies in an attractive setting with steep hills enclosing the sandy beach. In summer, visitors throng to its 2 km of east-facing sand. There is a usable strip of sand, but after exceptionally high tides the space for building sandcastles may be limited. Seek local advice on the location of rips before swimming. There is a boat-launching area at Blackhead, but in a high surf, launching can be difficult or impossible.

Because of the abundance of marine life in the Te Angiangi Marine Reserve, snorkelling and diving are popular in the area. Seek local advice on the best spots. Divers will find *Ecklonia* kelp forests offshore and a colourful display of fish species. At low tide paua and crayfish are often caught off the reefs at Blackhead. Surfcasters mainly catch kahawai, although fishing or taking of any marine life is forbidden within the boundaries of the Marine Reserve.

Artists find inspiration on the emancipating sands of North Island beaches.

Horses and 4WDs are permitted on the sand above the rocky platform, but not on the rocks below the high-water mark.

Quaint old-style baches and the rustic woolshed lend a yesteryear charm to Blackhead. The campground toilets are for public use.

To reach Blackhead from Waipukurau, follow Porangahau Road, then turn left into Wellington Road. Turn right into Tavistock Road, which becomes Farm Road. Keep left at the intersection with Middleton Road, 6 km from the town. Where Farm Road leads to Motere Road, keep left along Motere Road, which later becomes Long Range Road and leads all the way to Blackhead.

## Te Paerahi Beach, Porangahau

The expansive and wide vistas of Te Paerahi Beach stretch 16 km from Blackhead Point in the north to Porangahau Point in the south. The endless stretch of pristine sand provides one of the most magnificent sea views on the Hawke's Bay coast. To see the beach stretching to the distance in a haze of sea spray without a building or sign of human contact is

The wide expansive sands of Te Paerahi Beach stretch endlessly in a haze of salt spray to the distant headlands.

memorable. You feel small yet empowered on this fine beach, humbled by the vastness of the panorama.

The wide, gently shelving beach of firm golden sand is decorated with occasional pebbles and pipi shells. If you want to set up the cricket stumps or get the big hitters in to bat in a game of baseball, then this is the beach. Blokarters dream of a beach as open and wide as this.

Fishing is good all along the beach, especially for kahawai and snapper. The mouth of the Porangahau River is 8 km from the southern entrance and can only be reached by walking or boat. Kite fishing is popular here. Surfers enjoy the clean breakers and swimming is generally safe.

Blackhead Point was named by Captain Cook. As he sailed past in the *Endeavour*, the top of the cliffs appeared to be covered in a black line. This was a throng of Maori spectators watching the strange vessel passing by.

To access Te Paerahi Beach from Porangahau, follow Abercromby Street north until it turns sharp right into Dundas Street. This runs into Beach Road. There is also beach access along Te Paerahi Road through the pine trees.

From the north, a narrow coastal plain of pine forest and pasture shelters access to the beach until you get to Beach Road, 2.5 km from the settlement of Porangahau. Follow Beach Road until it meets the beach. There is a grass reserve with picnic tables, parking and toilets. The boat ramp is nearby. The small settlement has a campground, motor camp, accommodation and a store.

N

Taupo

L.
Taupo

L. 
Waikaremoana

Napier

Hastings

Whanganui R.

Wanganui

Mowhanau ⑨
Castlecliff ⑩

TASMAN SEA

Palmerston
North

Tangimoana ⑧⑨

Foxton Beach ⑧⑧

Waitarere Beach ⑧⑦

⑦② Herbertville

⑦③ Akitio

Otaki Beach ⑧⑥

Waikanae Beach ⑧⑤

Paraparaumu Beach ⑧④
Paekakariki ⑧③

Masterton

⑦④ Castlepoint Beach
⑦⑤ Deliverance Cove

Plimmerton ⑧②

Titahi Bay ⑧①

⑦⑥ Riversdale Beach

Makara Beach ⑧⑩

WELLINGTON

L.
Wairarapa

⑦⑨

Owhiro Bay

⑦⑦ Tora

PACIFIC OCEAN

⑦⑧
Cape Palliser

# Wairarapa

The Wairarapa coastline is a jumbled mix of fine sandy beaches and raw stretches of rocky coast. Some beaches such as Akitio and Riversdale Beach are small seaside settlements behind golden sandy strips. Others like Herbertville are on an enormous scale, stretching to distant headlands in a curtain of salt spray.

At Castlepoint, unique rock formations capped by the majestic lighthouse have sculpted a rugged backdrop to the beaches. Further south at Tora and Cape Palliser, the Wairarapa coast becomes more untamed and savage.

High cliffs tumble unabated to narrow stretches of flat land at the coast. Monstrous waves batter the coastal rocks, culminating in orgies of foam. Fierce winds whip the froth into swirling maelstroms. Fur seals frequent the scattered rocks of the promontories. These are beaches where you come to admire the power of the coast, not to swim or sunbathe.

All the Wairarapa beaches are around 50 km from SH2. The roads are often unsealed and pass through huge inland sheep stations. Campgrounds are located at some beaches, but Castlepoint, Riversdale and Akitio are the only settlements with services.

The climate of the Wairarapa is warm and dry in summer and prone to strong winds. The drama of the coast is best illustrated in adverse weather.

## Herbertville

Herbertville is named after Joseph and Sarah Herbert, who arrived in New Zealand aboard the *London*. They settled the district in 1834 and left their legacy in the name of the settlement.

You can visit their memorial a few kilometres past the settlement of Herbertville. The main access to the beach is right beside the memorial, although it is little more than an overgrown 4WD track. Park by the litter bins on the bumpy grass reserves and make your own way over 30 metres of dunes. Other accessways are further south.

Before the settlement, the road forks; left runs along Tuatare Road and right leads to the beach along Seaview Road. Heading south along Seaview Road you pass Burnview Station with its grand two-storey homestead, complete with verandahs and a turret.

The enormous beach is 14 km long and composed of reddy-brown sand. It is wide and expansive with a grand setting. The profile between the shore and dunes forms a gentle hump, which is soft to walk on when wet by the outgoing tide. An ankle-deep lagoon on the landward side of the beach sometimes forms, and is frequented by black-backed gulls and oystercatchers. Occasional large driftwood trunks lie dormant on the beach, waiting for the next storm to push them further up the dunes.

At the northern end of the beach, the imposing south face of Cape Turnagain's fluted cliffs forms a dramatic backdrop. Cape Turnagain was named by Captain Cook in 1769. On arriving in New Zealand near present-day Gisborne, Cook needed to find shelter and water. He sailed south and having found no place to harbour or take on provisions, he decided to turn around and head north.

One of Cook's missions on his voyage aboard the *Endeavour* was to discover the great unknown southern land, *'terra australis incognita'*. Scientists of the day believed it must exist to balance the weight of the Northern Hemisphere continents, otherwise the world would surely topple over. Four months later, having circumnavigated New Zealand, Cook recognised Cape Turnagain and thus established that New Zealand was not the great unknown southern continent.

There is no walking access around the cape. However, if you turn left into Tuatare Road at the road fork before Herbertville and continue 2.4 km to a gate (just on the far side of Tuatare River bridge), you can access the beach to launch your boat near the cape. Seek local advice for the best place on the beach to launch. You will need a 4WD. There is no beach access along Tuatare Road.

On the beach you can fish for kahawai or use the huge space for a game of cricket or frisbee. The sand may be too soft for blokarting. Seek local advice on where to swim. The local pub is your best bet for finding activity among the otherwise sleepy collection of baches.

Herbertville has a campground, store and pub. It is reached by following Herbertville Road 10 km from Wimbledon. Wimbledon is 21 km from Weber and 56 km from Dannevirke.

# Akitio

The beach at Akitio stretches 2 km, from the Akitio River mouth at the northern end to rocks at the southern end. At the boat club the beach curves gently around a point, with a campground nearby. South of the campground there is no beach access. North of the boat club, Akitio's Esplanade is separated from the beach by a narrow grass reserve. There is a boat ramp near the boat club with a parking area.

Akitio's narrow strip of sand is tinged red and firm to walk on. Around the point it becomes more strewn with kelp and driftwood. The beach shelves gently and is generally safe for swimming. Surfers and boogie-boarders enjoy the clean breaks of the waves.

There is a notable reef very close to the shore, which you can almost walk out to at low tide. It's a popular place for snorkelling or diving for paua and crayfish. The best fishing is at the mouth of the Akitio River. You can explore the lower reaches of the Akitio River by kayak. Paddle a few kilometres upstream to view the grand old homesteads by the bridge.

The remains of Akitio's pier still protrude through the water, just south of the public toilets. Akitio's campground has a store and a fish-and-chip shop is nearby.

To reach Akitio from Dannevirke, follow Miller Street to Weber Road and continue 35 km to Weber. Just 1 km south of Weber turn right onto SH 52. Akitio is signposted 8 km further on at Waione along River Road. This becomes Coast Road at the bridge over the Akitio River.

From the south, follow Pahiatua–Pongaroa Road from 2.5 km north of Pahiatua on SH2. At Rakaunui turn left to Pongaroa and follow Coast Road to Akitio.

# Castlepoint Beach

Castlepoint Beach has a northerly aspect, with stunning views up the Wairarapa coastline. There is a charming lighthouse standing solemnly on Castle Point.

At the western end the sand shelves gently to a generally calm surf, and provides safe swimming. There is a strip of dry golden sand above the high-tide mark, which is good for sunbathing or building sandcastles. Surfers enjoy the beach on a northerly swell.

Towards the eastern end, the beach becomes rocky. A protective rock wall has been constructed to stop the road and houses behind being washed away by the encroaching sea. At low tide you can walk all the way to the neck of sand between Castlepoint Beach and Deliverance Cove.

From the neck of sand at the eastern end you can take a walk over the wooden footbridge to Castlepoint Lighthouse. This 30-minute-return walk on a concrete track also has wooden boardwalks to protect the fossilised limestone underneath. The lighthouse was constructed in England in 1913. The steel sections were bolted together to form the 23-metre-high tower. The light flashes every 30 seconds and has a range of 48 km. You can look all the way along 'The Reef' to Castle Rock from the summit of Castle Point.

Watch for yellow-eyed penguins around the rocks. Australasian gannets, black shags and white-fronted terns sometimes circle on the updraughts.

Every March the locals hold a horse race along the beach. Betting truly is a lottery, as you don't know which horse your money's on until the race has started.

Castlepoint has a motor camp, store and motel accommodation. Parking and public toilets are behind the beach and at the parking area at the end of Jetty Road.

Castlepoint is 64 km from Masterton. Take Te Ore Ore Road from northbound SH2.

## Deliverance Cove

Deliverance Cove is sheltered by 'The Reef', an outcrop of fossil-rich limestone which runs around the seaward edge of the bay in a gentle arc to Castle Rock. It forms a bulbous lagoon, the shape of a fishing boat fender, which meets a narrow neck of sand at its northern end below Castle Point.

The scenically stunning and idyllic cove is well sheltered from wind and wave. It is ideal for swimming with young children. Its fine golden sand is enclosed in a bowl, with dunes covered in pingao and spinifex rising to a ridge that encircles the cove.

The mouth of the reef is open and you can watch the fishing boats exit through this natural gateway to the ocean. Standing sentinel at the southern gate is the imposing 160-metre peak of Castle Rock. It was named in 1770 by Captain Cook, who thought the jagged outcrop resembled the battlements of a castle.

A track leads to the summit from the southern end of the beach. Alternatively, follow the Deliverance Cove Track signs from the carpark at the end of Jetty Road. The walk takes approximately 1½ hours return and follows a steep but well-formed track. You can see the worn grass track through the windswept grass while standing on the beach. Follow it to the summit and on windy days beware of rogue gusts. The wind accelerates up the face and can gust ferociously. On the beach it can be calm, while on the summit it is blowing a gale. Look at the grass to see the gusts tracing invisible lines across the grass. The reward for the climb is superb views of Deliverance Cove, 'The Reef' and Castlepoint Lighthouse.

Beware of sunbathing fur seals on the grass dunes at the water's edge. If you should chance an encounter, keep well away and stay on the landward side.

On the beach you can watch the breakers froth over low points in 'The Reef' and spout white water plumes through embryonic blowholes. 'The Reef' is a popular fishing spot, but heed the warning signs concerning the deaths and injuries that have occurred through freak waves.

There are toilets, picnic tables and a carpark at Castlepoint Scenic Reserve at the end of Jetty Road. Castlepoint has a store and motor camp.

Deliverance Cove is 64 km east of Masterton at Castlepoint. It is comprehensively signposted along Te Ore Ore Road from northbound SH2 in Masterton.

## Riversdale Beach

Riversdale is a sleepy seaside community set on a 3 km stretch of golden sand. The beach is popular with families and generally safe for swimming, although there are occasional cross-currents.

The Surf Life Saving Club is at the northern end of the beach by the lagoon. Over the summer months, the Surf Life Saving Club is very active with a 'nippers' programme for pre-schoolers and youngsters to learn about water safety. The introduction sets them up for future training as lifeguards. At Easter a 'Junior Jaws' fishing contest is held for youngsters to catch the ugliest or smelliest fish in the lagoon.

The hub of the community is the village store near the northern end of the beach. It also serves takeaway meals and has petrol pumps. Nearby is an attractive walkway beneath the pines at the mouth of the river. This is a good spot to find some shade and have a picnic. The village also has a golf course, tennis courts and campground.

You can walk all the way along the beach on a wide strip of dry sand. Another reserve at the southern end of the beach has boat-launching facilities and picnic tables. Surfing and boogie-boarding are popular.

Around 25 years ago an elephant seal named 'Jumbo' visited Riversdale and stayed a few months. He would lumber up the streets and park himself by cars. He became a local icon and is still remembered in postcards at the local store.

Riversdale is 54 km from Masterton. Follow Te Ore Ore from northbound SH2 in Masterton and follow the signposts at Awatoitoi.

## Tora

The coastline around Tora is not for rolling out your towel to sunbathe. It is better suited to admiring nature's majesty. This is an untamed stretch of coast with a wild and raw feel to it.

Surfers flock to Tora for its notorious big wave breaks. There are several breaks along the beach and you can always be a spectator while eating your picnic.

Imposing craggy cliffs cascade to a narrow base of flat pasture. The coastal vistas, exposed rocky hillsides and parched windswept grass are the source of inspiration for painters and photographers. When there is a swell, you can while away the time watching the waves crash violently over the offshore rocks.

When wind comes from a westerly direction, it can funnel ferociously through the gullies and peel off a foaming crest of spray from the incoming waves. You can sit and watch the unfolding of nature from any of the reserves lining the coastline. Some have toilets, and informal camping is permitted in specified areas.

The road splits just before Tora; left takes you north to Te Awaiti, right leads to Tora. Sandy Bay, along the road to Te Awaiti, is the only stretch of sand, but it is quite coarse. At the mouth of the Oterei River to the north, there is a shingle beach between the lagoon and sea, but it is steeply shelving.

There is limited accommodation at Tora. Te Awaiti has a sprinkling of baches and there is boat-launching at Sandy Bay. A coastal walk is organised by a group of local farming families.

South towards Tora you can look at the rusting bulldozers used to launch the commercial fishing boats. Some abandoned hulks of machinery are left in their final resting place above the beach. Further south is the rotting bow section and boiler of a shipwrecked hull, rusting and being gnawed incessantly by the waves. They give testimony to the wild nature of the coast.

The old shearing shed at the southern end of the beach is also worth a look for the textures on its decaying iron. This artefact of Wairarapa farming history blends perfectly into its setting.

To reach Tora from Martinborough, follow White Rock Road for 1.8 km and turn left into Blackridge Road. Follow it 31 km to Tuturumuri and turn left into Tora Road just over the bridge past the school. Tora is a further 14 km.

A rusting bulldozer lies in its final resting place on the wild and windswept beach at Tora.

# Cape Palliser

The North Island's most southerly beach is a small stretch of black shingle, pounded on one side by monstrous waves and guarded on the other by the lighthouse at Cape Palliser.

You can take a walk to the lighthouse from the gravel parking bay at the road-end. The climb up the 258 steps takes approximately ten minutes. The light station was set up in 1897 and in 1959 was converted from oil to diesel-generated electricity. From 1967 its 1000-watt bulb was powered by mains electricity. The tower is 18 metres high and constructed from cast iron sections bolted together. It stands 78 metres above sea level.

The perpetual crashing of the waves, and their explosion into bursts of foam on the offshore rocks, are an awesome display. Water cascades off the rocks in rivulets and mini waterfalls. Fragments of the waves are held in mid-air by fierce winds, which fuel the aquatic fireworks display. Frothing maelstroms of swirling water advance and retreat on the steeply shelving pebbles. This is the North Island's coastline at its wildest. Don't swim.

A colony of fur seals breeds on the rocks at Cape Palliser. They can sometimes be seen sleeping and sunbathing on rocks. Stay landward side and keep dogs under control. The colony at Cape Palliser is the North Island's largest breeding population. When not in the water feeding on squid and fish, they rest on land, using their flippers like radiators to cool themselves down. They are insulated by a layer of blubber beneath a fur coat, which protects them from the sometimes extreme conditions they encounter.

The drive to Cape Palliser is 37 km along Whatarangi Road, which is on the left before reaching Lake Ferry. Some 5 km before Cape Palliser you pass Ngawi, a small fishing village with a line of fishing boats above the beach. Tractors are not powerful enough to haul the fishing boats up the steeply shelving beach, so bulldozers are the norm. They come in all shapes, sizes and states of disrepair.

The road is both sealed and unsealed. Active erosion threatens some sections and, in places, it is perched right above a furious frothing sea. The nearest store is at Lake Ferry.

Cape Palliser was named by Captain Cook after his mentor, Admiral Sir Hugh Palliser.

The lighthouse at Cape Palliser stands over the North Island's most southerly beach.

# Wellington and Kapiti

Beaches around Wellington are few and far between. Heading north along SH1, you first encounter sand at Titahi Bay and Plimmerton. Titahi Bay, with its charming collection of boatsheds, and Plimmerton, with its stately beachside properties, both have the feel of English seaside towns.

From Paekakariki north the beaches run in an almost continuous sequence all the way to Wanganui, punctuated only by occasional rivers, streams and rocky outcrops. This coast was formerly known as the 'Beach Road'. At Paekakariki, Cobb and Co. carriages would descend to the beach and use the almost unbroken stretches of sand as the main communications route. Coaches would only stop at accommodation houses near river mouths.

From Paekakariki, Kapiti Island comes into view and then dominates the coastal views until north of Waikanae. This world-famous nature reserve is a haven for endangered birds and has an aura about it that pervades the beaches of the area. Sunsets, with the dark profile of Kapiti Island in the foreground, are memorable and well worth enjoying with a picnic on a warm summer evening.

Most beach towns are well developed and cater to holiday-makers. The summers are generally warm and dry, but winter and spring may be showery.

## Owhiro Bay

Nestled on the south-western side of Wellington Harbour, Owhiro Bay is a small outpost of the city that has a village feel. A collection of quaint houses line the roadside, which runs above the gravel and rocky beach.

You can look across the mouth of the harbour to the lighthouse at Pencarrow Head. This was the first lighthouse in New Zealand and was in use from 1859–1906, before the lower light was built. Ferries roll into the harbour and aeroplanes fight the winds to land at the nearby airport. You can see the South Island to the west on a clear day.

From the western road-end at Owhiro you can park and take a two-hour-return walk to Sinclair Head via Red Rocks. These red-stained rocks were formed around 200 million years ago during an undersea volcanic eruption. On contact with the water, the lava cooled rapidly and formed pillow shapes. These structures are well preserved. One Maori legend says the red colour came from the blood of Maui's nose. He used this as bait to fish up Te-Ika-a-Maui (the North Island).

At Sinclair Head there is a colony of fur seals, who use the rocks as a haul-out site over winter to condition themselves for the breeding season. You can observe them sunbathing, sleeping and scratching. Keep dogs under control and always stay landward side.

On the walk you pass an assortment of beautifully preserved old-style baches. Some have rockeries in their gardens and brightly painted walls and roofs. If there were ever a museum for baches there would be many exhibits from this selection.

New Zealand fur seals are a relatively common sight on the southern beaches of the North Island.

Owhiro Bay is reached from central Wellington by following signs to Island Bay and then following The Esplanade west. Boat-launching facilities are located at the northern end of Owhiro Bay.

## Makara Beach

Makara Beach is a desolate and windswept cove, buffeted by frequent gales. Its short, steeply shelving gravel beach faces north and is hemmed in by steep hills.

To the north, the hills have occasional baches scattered at their feet. To the south the hills can be explored via the Makara Walkway.

This three-hour-return walk heads steeply inland for 45 minutes and follows the top of the ridge to some World War Two gun emplacements. It is easy to understand why this site was chosen because the views north past Mana Island, and west to Marlborough, stretch endlessly to the horizon.

The track descends via a steep, disused, metalled road and follows the rocky coastline for the final 1½ hours. This scenic and dramatic coastline is strewn with driftwood, seaweed and shell fragments. The inland section is closed from 1 August to 31 October for lambing, and dogs are only permitted along the coastal section of the walk.

At the eastern end of the beach is Makara Reserve, a fenced area containing a rare collection of indigenous coastal plants. These form a community that is now rare in the Wellington region. The ground-hugging plants of note are *Pimelia*, a snaking accretion of spongy dark-green leaflets; and *Raoulia*, a mat of triangular pale-green leaflets. Both withstand the wind, salt desiccation and sand-blasting of the harsh environment.

Makara Beach is reached via Makara Road, 10 km from Karori. It has a store, café and toilets.

## Titahi Bay

Titahi Bay is a charming seaside holiday spot, reminiscent of an old English-style beach destination of the 'Oh I do like to be beside the seaside' variety. Its quaint proportions and the lines of brightly painted boatsheds lend a cosy and nostalgic feel to the bay.

The bay developed primarily as a resort for wealthy Wellingtonians. In the late 1920s and 1930s, prominent residents of Titahi Bay tried to promote the sandy beach as a holiday destination. During the Depression it became a popular spot, where the problems and politics of the day could be forgotten. Many old photos depict lines of cars along the arc of the beach, and people in woollen bathing costumes enjoying its crescent of sand.

Most of the boatsheds were built between 1950 and 1953. Previously a report by a building inspector described existing sheds as 'an eyesore; there is not one that does not need painting or repairs'. Today the sheds form another aesthetic focus for the bay. Some are brightly painted, others more rusticated. Some even have satellite dishes. There is an annual tug–of–war competition between owners of sheds at the northern and southern ends.

During summer, the 'Big Dig' is held at the northern end of the beach. Holiday-makers search for buried 'treasure' to win prizes. The whole occasion has an atmosphere of festivity.

Most of the rusticated boat sheds at Titahi Bay were constructed in the 1950s.

Access is off Bay Road at the northern end and off Tirets Road at the southern end. Both have toilets near the beach access. Picnic tables line the beach. There is parking at the northern and southern ends. Vehicles are permitted on both ends of the beach for boat-launching and access to the boatsheds.

The beach is popular with surfers. It is gently shelving and safe for swimming, with a Surf Life Saving Club. Fishermen enjoy the rocks at both headlands.

Mana Island lies 2.5 km offshore. According to Maori legend the distinctive shape was caused by Te Awarua o Porirua, the taniwha of Porirua Harbour. While learning to fly, he crashed and cut off the top of the island. In European times the island was given over to farming. In 1973 it became a nature reserve and is now administered by DoC. You can visit if you have a boat, but read the signs posted at the northern end of the beach concerning restrictions.

Titahi Bay is 21 km north of Wellington. It faces north and still thrives as a summer holiday destination. It is still the closest sandy beach to Wellington. There are shops, cafés and accommodation nearby.

## Plimmerton

Plimmerton's beaches start at South Beach, which is at the southern end of the same sandy bay as Plimmerton Beach. Heading north around the headland, where the fire station is located, is Sunset Parade, with its innumerable rock pools. Karehana Bay is a small sandy enclave at the northern end. Around the headland with the wharf and boat club is Hongoeka Bay.

Plimmerton developed as a seaside town for wealthy Wellingtonians to visit. When the railway to Palmerston North was completed in 1886, Plimmerton became more accessible. It quickly became established as a popular holiday town and was marketed as the 'Brighton of the South Seas'. Its name comes from John Plimmer, who was a company director of the Wellington and Manawatu Railway Company. Plimmerton certainly retains an air of Englishness and has the feel of Blackpool, Bournemouth or Brighton.

You can walk along the promenade from Beach Road, along Sunset Parade to Moana Road and admire the eclectic mix of architectural styles. They show the complete spectrum of New Zealand seaside architecture, from wooden weatherboard guest houses to newer plaster-coated mansions.

Plimmerton is a place to get back to the simple pleasures. You can unpack a picnic or fly your kite. People often play petanque on the sandy parts of the beach. The rock pools alongside Sunset Parade are popular with local school groups. Because of its sheltered aspect and gently shelving profile, the beach is popular for swimming with both the elderly and young families. Fishing from the wharf at the boat club is also popular.

You can bring your kayak and paddle out to the rock gardens in the centre of the bay. More experienced paddlers can make a day trip to Mana Island, but seek local advice before attempting this trip.

South Beach is popular with windsurfers. A web camera is positioned on the boat club so windsurfers can always monitor the conditions.

You can walk along the 500 metres of South Beach and imagine the views open to beachfront residents. Beachfront takes on a new meaning here, with concrete walls built to protect the fronts of sections. At king tides the waves break right against the walls.

Access to South Beach is via two side-roads with parking from Beach Road. There are toilets on the southern side of the headland that separates Plimmerton's main beach from South Beach.

## Paekakariki

Paekakariki Beach is a low-key beach used frequently by locals but visited little by holiday-makers.

Marine Parade runs almost the entire 4 km of the beach, but access near the southern end is limited. On most tides the sea meets a protective seawall, which helps dissipate the erosive power of the waves, making this section of beach unusable.

The Surf Life Saving Club at the northern end has toilets and parking. It is the best place to swim, as the beach is prone to occasional rips and undertows.

By far the best access to the beach is at the northern end through Queen Elizabeth Park. The park is open from 8 a.m. to 6 p.m. and well-furnished with toilets, picnic tables and changing sheds. Refer to the information panels for access to the beach, as the park is connected to the beach via short tracks over the dunes. The park has a network of coastal walking tracks that weave through the mature dunes. Despite modification by humans, fire and invasive weeds, the dunes represent fine examples of native plant succession. Near the sea are sand-collecting plants such as pingao, taupata and sand coprosma. Higher up, on the established dunes, are sand-binding species such as bracken, ngaio and flax.

You can take a two-hour-return walk through the park to Whareroa Beach and Raumati. The track is wide, metalled and even. Refer to the information panels for accessways to the beach so you can return along the beach.

The beach is good for shell-collecting. You can surfcast from the tea-coloured sand, with Kapiti Island dominating the view at the northern end, and Marlborough visible to the south on a clear day.

Paekakariki has shops, a backpackers, accommodation and a motor camp.

A local poet wrote about his beach with these words:

From *Three Paekakariki fragments*, by Michael O'Leary

> as dusk darkened
> the surrounding hills
> looked like they were
> folding towards the beach
> the sky, thick clouded,
> mirrored the choppy
> waves which quietly rolled
> onto the black sand
> and something alien
> caught my vision
> a large, black pointed fin
> beyond the white breakers
> but near enough to
> the shore to hear me
> talking to it. Later
> I told people that
> I took my pet shark
> for a walk tonight.

# Paraparaumu Beach

Paraparaumu Beach is the most developed beach resort town in the vicinity of Wellington. Backing on to its wide stretch of sand around Maclean Park are shops, restaurants, cafés and motels. The boat club is at the northern end of the park, from where charter boats take visitors to Kapiti Island.

Kapiti Island is the emblem of the district and gives its name to the coastal region it shelters. The island is a famous reserve for endangered birds and can only be visited with a permit from DoC. Rare bird species you would not normally encounter on the mainland such as saddleback, stitchbird and takahe roam free in Kapiti's predator-free environment. A marine reserve also spans the area to the north of Paraparaumu Beach and is demarcated with white markers on land and buoys at sea.

Maori were attracted to the area from around AD 1100 and were lured by the abundance of seafood on the coast and the high number of birds inhabiting the inland swamps.

Following Captain Cook's visit to Entry Anchorage on Kapiti Island in 1770, the area became charted. From the 1830s, whalers used the coast and Kapiti Island as a launching point. When the railway from Wellington to Palmerston North was completed in 1886 the area became accessible for development. This expansion continues today and the coast is still being enjoyed by locals and holiday-makers.

The best access to Paraparaumu Beach is at Maclean Park, where there are children's play areas, picnic tables and parking by the services of the town. The area is famous for its sunsets, so evening is a good time to bring

Sunset from Paraparaumu Beach with the dark silhouette of Kapiti Island in the foreground.

a picnic and watch the nightly display of colour behind the gentle contours of Kapiti Island.

The area is generally safe for swimming, being sheltered by Kapiti Island and having a gently shelving beach profile. Successive sandbanks trap bodies of warm water, so expect temperature variations as you swim out. An annual swimming race is held from Rangatira on Kapiti Island to Paraparaumu Beach.

The beach is sometimes matted with debris from the outflow of Waikanae Estuary, but the tea-coloured sand is generally clean. You can find pieces of driftwood and decorate them with toetoe stalks and flax flowers from the beach, then stand them up to make totem poles. Watch for vehicles, which sometimes use the beach as a highway. Boat-launching usually takes place at the boat club near Maclean Park.

Maclean Park is at the junction of Marine Parade and Manly Street. It is reached from SH1 via Kapiti Road, which skirts the airport and golf course.

South of Maclean Park along Marine Parade, there is roadside parking and picnic tables, with accessways to the beach. North along Manly Street, lines of houses are situated between the beach and road. Occasional accessways and roadside parking lead to quieter parts of the beach.

## Waikanae Beach

Most of the views of Waikanae Beach are hidden behind residential areas. The best access is from Waimea Domain, between Rangihiroa Street and Hemara Street. There are toilets, a café, store and play area. A large grassed area is shaded with trees if you need a break from the beach.

From here you can explore the beach in both directions and take a walk looking for shellfish in the tea-coloured sand. The Waimea Stream flows to the beach a little north of the Domain. Just south of the creek, off Field Way, is another accessway with a nearby toilet. Swimming in or near the river mouth is discouraged due to the water quality. The boat ramp is located at the boat club before Waimea Road public toilets.

South of Waimea Domain you will need to turn into one of the side roads to access the beach. There is access and parking at Ara Kuaka, Oratia Street, Stonewall Grove and Te Moana Road.

At the southern end of the beach is Waimanu Lagoon. The coastline of the nearby Waikanae Estuary is incorporated into the Kapiti Marine Reserve. You can see an abundance of birdlife here, including black swans, pied stilts and flocks of black-backed gulls. Outflow from the waterway does not meet public health guidelines, so don't swim, fish or take shellfish. Taking of marine life is prohibited in the Marine Reserve.

North of Waimea Domain there are occasional accessways with roadside parking on Field Way. North of Field Way is the quietest stretch of beach, so if you are looking for solitude, head here. In 1954 the trawler *Phyllis* ran aground at the northern end of the beach. Today her remains are covered by sand.

During the summer Waikanae is a busy beach, but is quieter during winter months. It is often sheltered by Kapiti Island, but less so than Paraparaumu. Waikanae is a lower-key beach than its more showy neighbour. It has a calmer feel and is less developed.

The first subdivision in Waikanae was in 1913, when W. Field sold 105 sections. A drive along Tutere Road and Field Way, or a walk along the beach, shows the whole range of New Zealand beachside buildings, from 1950s baches to 1990s 'Santa Fe' replicas.

Although the winds are calmer than further south, windsurfers use the prevailing onshore northwesterly wind. The coast can be good for slalom and longboard sailing.

Pekapeka Beach is 5 km north of Waikanae along SH1. It is signposted along Pekapeka Road and has a parking area with vehicle access to the beach. The beach is often deserted, but lacks the shelter from Kapiti Island. It is a good place for solitude or building shacks from driftwood logs. The beach doesn't have the appeal of Waikanae but is joined along the same stretch of sand.

## Otaki Beach

Otaki Beach is a quiet and laid-back beach of metallic grey sand. The beach is a good place for collecting shells, especially cockles. Numerous shells are sprinkled among the driftwood, which is plentiful at the base of the dunes.

Swimming is generally safe and there is a Surf Life Saving Club. Avoid swimming at the southern end of the beach and at the mouth of Otaki River, where there is a strong undertow.

The mouth of the river is a good place to fish for kahawai and blue cod. Its braided course is one of the main drains of the western side of the Tararuas, and a large gravel area has formed at the river mouth. To reach the mouth of the Otaki River, continue along Marine Parade and veer right on to the gravel banks. The vehicle track is well-formed but rough.

A ferry was stationed here when the beaches were used as a carriage route before the advent of the Wellington to Palmerston North railway in 1886.

Main access to the beach is along Tasman Road from SH1. Most services are located on the main highway and in the village, 3 km before the beach. The reserve by the beach has ample parking, toilets, picnic tables and barbecues. There is vehicle access for boat-launching. There is one accessway north of Tasman Road Reserve.

South from the reserve along Marine Parade there are no accessways over the dunes. Near the junction with Rangiuru Road is a rock cairn, which commemorates the wrecks of the *Felixstowe* and *City of Auckland*, both wrecked in 1878.

# Wanganui and Manawatu

From Otaki north to Wanganui, the coast is characterised by long sweeping beaches that arc gently to form a large bay. The endless stretches of tea-coloured sand are decorated with pipi and cockle shells. The rivers that drain the Tararua Range punctuate the beaches, and wide river mouths, abundant with birdlife and shellfish, are popular places for fishing. Between the beach and Tararuas lies a fertile alluvial strip, which merges with large dune fields near the beaches.

Most beaches are accessed by heading seaward a few kilometres through farmland from SH1. The hummocky terrain of some farmland indicates the area was formerly a dune field. Some well-preserved areas of dune occur on the coast and there are numerous ecological restoration projects to safeguard the first line of defence against the sea.

The coastline between Paekakariki and Wanganui used to carry Cobb and Co. carriages along what was known as the 'Beach Road'. Accommodation houses and stables were situated at river mouths to shelter travellers when river levels were high. The 'Beach Road' was made redundant in the late 1880s when the Wellington to Palmerston North railway was completed. This also had the effect of opening up the region for development and making the beaches more accessible for recreational use.

The coast is steeped in Maori history. Haunui-a-nanaia was the son of Ropoto, leader of the *Kurahaupo* canoe. Hau's wife Wairaka had run off with her lover Weku and headed south from Taranaki to Pukerua. As Hau followed her in pursuit, he named the prominent rivers. These were later recorded in a lullaby.

Many of the beaches have a desolate and expansive feel. Most sand is tea-coloured and covered in driftwood.

## Waitarere Beach

Waitarere Beach is a 10 km stretch of beach that runs from Hokio Stream in the south to the Manawatu River mouth in the north. It is a long sweeping beach that runs to the horizon in both directions, backed by low spinifex-covered dunes. Either side of the settlement there are pine plantations.

The sleepy settlement of Waitarere has a store, restaurant, takeaway and motor camp. Main access to the beach is along Waitarere Beach Road, 7.5 km north of Levin and 11 km south of Foxton. Where the road meets the beach, there is vehicle access, although boat-launching may be difficult due to the artificial chicane put in the road access. Turn right at the signpost just before the beach to a carpark with toilets and changing sheds. There is also a Surf Life Saving Club and information on the *Hydrabad* wreck, which lies approximately 2 km to the south.

The *Hydrabad* was a cotton-trading ship, built in Scotland in 1865. On 24 June 1878, when bound from Lyttelton to Adelaide, gale-force winds and heavy seas drove the ship ashore. When the captain ordered the anchors to be dropped, the huge swell ruptured the cables and she ran aground. All 33 people aboard survived. The wreck now lies partially exposed and parallel to the beach, its bow facing north. It is tilted towards the sea and mostly filled with sand, but the hull remains intact. The rusting bow and stern sections and ribs of the hull protrude through the sand and still give a good impression of the size of the vessel.

Heading south from Waitarere Beach along Rua Avenue there are other accessways to the beach. To cut down your walking time to the wreck site, you can follow Rua Avenue and turn right into Hydrabad Drive, then walk

The wreck of the *Hydrabad* lies solemnly on the sands of Waitarere Beach.

south along the beach. The walk takes approximately 15 minutes each way from Hydrabad Avenue. Add approximately 30 minutes each way from the Surf Life Saving Club.

Vehicles are permitted on the beach and horse-riding is popular along the kilometres of unbroken sand. The dune area is undergoing ecological restoration, so use of any vehicles on the dune areas is not permitted.

Hokio Stream forms the southern boundary of the beach. Hokio Beach has toilets, barbecues and picnic tables and is accessed from Hokio Beach Road, 1.5 km south of Levin. The road-end is set back a little from the beach, and access to the beach is via a walk over the low dunes, crowned with tufts of spinifex. The beach at Hokio is less attractive than at Waitarere, but is more desolate and undiscovered.

Hau (see introduction to the Wanganui and Manawatu sections) named the area around Hokio during pursuit of his runaway wife. When he heard a noise above him, he thought it came from a giant invisible bird called Hokio.

In 1858 the Cobb and Co. carriage between Wanganui and Wellington travelled the 'Beach Road'. Hector McDonald built an accommodation house and stables at the mouth of the Hokio Stream. This was in existence until 1886, when the railway was completed.

## Foxton Beach

The Manawatu Estuary is the most important estuarine habitat in the lower North Island, with over 35 species recorded around the fertile waters. You can see arctic wading birds such as bar-tailed godwits and lesser knots. South Island breeders, such as South Island pied oystercatchers and wrybills, also inhabit the area. Many birds are also local residents such as the royal spoonbill, New Zealand shoveler and pied stilt.

You can take a walk south from the carpark to the mouth of the Manawatu River. The walk takes around 30 minutes each way, but at the mouth of the estuary you will need to take care as around high tide the waves break near the dunes. Manawatu was named by Hau, 'manawa' meaning 'heart' and 'tatu' meaning 'to stumble'.

A band of driftwood is scattered at the base of steep dunes along the beach, and around high tide you will need to pick your way through the obstacle course. You can build beach shacks with the logs or look for ornamental pieces to restore and display at home.

The area around the mouth of the Manawatu River was originally settled because of the large flax swamp, which also provided an abundance of eels for the Maori community. Later, when the Crimean War broke out in the 1850s, there was a large demand for flax, which was needed for rope-making. This trade in flax continued until the early 1900s and the settlement thrived. Foxton Beach was always the staging post for goods produced in Palmerston North, which became the dominant settlement in the region.

Foxton Beach is signposted from Foxton, just north of the town centre. Follow Robinson Street, which turns into Foxton Beach Road for 5 km. Foxton Beach has shops, cafés, motor camps and motels.

Foxton Beach has a Surf Life Saving Club at the end of Ocean Beach Road, which also has substantial parking areas, picnic tables and toilets. The beach is accessed via a steep bank and aided with steps. For boat-launching, head north at the roundabout near the Surf Life Saving Club and follow the road 200 metres through the dunes.

The beach stretches north through the distant haze past Himatangi Beach to the mouth of the Rangitikei River nearly 20 km away at Tangimoana. It is possible to drive 4WDs from Foxton Beach via Himatangi to Tangimoana.

Himatangi is 7 km from SH1 along Himatangi Beach Road and has a Surf Life Saving Club, café, shop and motor camp. It's a sleepy seaside settlement, mostly hidden from the beach by high dunes, and the only opening to the beach is by the stream. The main access to the beach is by the Surf Life Saving Club, which also has toilets. Parking is on the beach at the mouth of the Kaikokopu Stream.

Fishing is popular all along the beach and, as vehicles and horses are permitted on the beach, there is nothing to stop you finding an isolated place away from accessways. Seek local advice on conditions before driving on the beach.

## Tangimoana

The settlement of Tangimoana has stayed small and never developed like other seaside towns. The beach is wild and untouched. Save a few pine trees, there is no evidence of human modifcation.

The beach is approximately 1.5 km from the settlement and is accessed along Tangimoana Beach Road and through extensive dune fields. There is a parking area, but no other facilities. This is the end of the 4WD track, which stretches all the way from Foxton Beach.

The carpark is at the mouth of the Rangitikei River. To access the beach you will need to walk for five minutes along the side of the river, where there is a shallow lagoon. The lagoon is a good place to swim with young children, and fishing is popular along the river and at the river mouth.

When land north of the river mouth was sold to the government in 1849, an accommodation house was set up by the Scott family. It was said to be the best lodging on the Wellington to Wanganui 'Beach Road' because it had glass windows. The Scott family also set up the ferry service.

Before World War Two the township was a popular holiday destination. In the mid-1930s, Gypsy Moth planes landed near the beach and often took locals on joyrides for 5 shillings. The river often floods, and in 1897 a huge lake was created, which destroyed the thriving port at the Rangitikei River mouth. In 1967 a cutting was constructed to divert it directly to the sea. The river was notorious for its movement, and between the 1920s and 1950s it caused part of the settlement to be moved several times.

Today Tangimoana is a quiet settlement with a motor camp and store. It has a sunny microclimate and is popular with windsurfers.

# Castlecliff

Castlecliff is the main beach for residents of Wanganui. It is the most southerly beach on the North Island's west coast that exhibits the characteristic black sand. Curiously, the beach at the southern jaw of the Whanganui River mouth has tea-coloured sand.

Being at the mouth of the North Island's second-largest river means the beach is covered with huge quantities of driftwood. It comes in all shapes and sizes. The beach is sometimes so choked with driftwood it is difficult to find a clear space to lay out your towel. You can often watch locals filling their trailers near the rock wall at the southern end of the beach.

A light is mounted on the man-made promontory to guide boats to the mouth of the river. According to Maori legend, the Whanganui River was formed when Mount Taranaki lost his fight with Mount Tongariro over the beautiful Mount Pihanga. He fled the central North Island, leaving a deep scar as he travelled seaward. Mount Tongariro healed the wound left by Mount Taranaki and formed the Whanganui River.

You can stand on the rock wall at the end of Morgan Street and look at the old dilapidated wharf on the opposite bank. The currents created by the discharge of water from the river stretch a long way out to sea.

The main area for beach users is at the end of Rangiora Street, where the Surf Life Saving Club is situated. There are huge parking areas that periodically become choked with sand. The westerly winds constantly blow it over the concrete barricade on the seaward side of the parking area, which was constructed to stop the problem. You can see bulldozers and diggers clearing the parking area, and also pushing mounds of driftwood logs to either end of the beach area. This is a perpetual operation.

Behind the Surf Life Saving Club is the Castlecliff Domain, a large grassed area with picnic tables and a huge children's play area. More parking is situated on the hill to the north of the Surf Life Saving Club. A network of tracks leaves from here, crisscrossing the dunes and offering shade and solitude. Where they head seaward you will often find the beach quieter. Watch for vehicles using the beach.

Kupe made Castlecliff one of his landfalls and named it 'Kai-hau-o-Kupe' – 'the place where Kupe ate nothing but wind'. Kupe continued his travels up the Whanganui River.

In 1885 the Wanganui Heads Railway Company started operating a service to Castlecliff. Passengers could visit the beach for a day trip to swim and fish. By the early 1900s the service was very popular and baches started to be built. In 1912 a tram service began and more people visited the beach.

From the northern end of the beach you can take a walk to Mowhanau. Follow the base of the cliffs and admire the grey papa rock slumping as it is chiselled away by the sea. The walk is on firm sand and only possible two hours either side of low tide. Near Mowhanau the cliffs protrude into the sea and are only negotiable when the water level is low. The walk takes approximately two hours one way. You can also drive a 4WD to Mowhanau, tide permitting.

## Mowhanau

The beach was once known as Kai Iwi, but was changed to Mowhanau to avoid confusion with the nearby settlement of Kai Iwi. At the mouth of Mowhanau Stream is a lagoon, which is good for young children to splash about in. A small bridge gives access to the best adventure playground you'll find anywhere.

The beach is an idyllic cove in the cliffs that stretch from Castlecliff to near Wainui. Its black sand takes on a purple tinge and occasional shells and pebbles ornament the surface. Driftwood is confined to the upper reaches of the stream by the lagoon, making the sand clean and good for laying out your towel. The beach is gently shelving and safe for swimming.

Rock pigeons dart in and out of holes in the low cliffs and kingfishers hover above the lagoon. White-faced herons and pied shags perch on the picturesque wooden footbridge, while gannets feed out to sea.

Next to the beach is a domain with toilets, parking, picnic tables and barbecues. Flax, taupata and pohutukawa surround the well-kept grass areas. There is a motor camp nearby.

On 11 January 1871 a Cobb and Co. coach service between Wanganui and New Plymouth commenced. The Old Coach Road, the only means of communication between Wanganui and northern settlements, passed through Mowhanau. After Rapanui, where horses were changed, the coach descended to the beach at Mowhanau and followed the coast to Okehu. The journey to New Plymouth usually took two days.

Take a walk around the southern headland past the mussel-encrusted rocks and admire the rock formations. Slabs of bluish-grey papa rock have slid from the main face to form offshore stacks, with rockeries of smooth stones ornamenting their base. The southern headland is only negotiable two hours either side of low tide.

You can continue the walk all the way to Castlecliff near Wanganui. The walk takes two hours one way. You should aim to arrive at Castlecliff no later than three hours after low tide, earlier if a big swell is prevalent. Seek local advice if you are in doubt. The walk follows the base of the cliffs along firm sand. If tides permit 4WDs can also travel along the beach to Castlecliff.

You can also take a 20-minute-return walk north along the beach. After five minutes you come to an elaborate footbridge over the Kai Iwi Stream. Follow the path up the hill. On the descent along the road you can look up to the southern headland and see the remains of the Old Coach Road. A redoubt was situated on the southern hills above the beach and was used in the 1860s Land Wars. Alexander's Redoubt was one of the main fortifications in the area used to defend Wanganui.

At the mouth of the Mowhanau Stream you can see the remains of an old World War Two gun emplacement that used to be stationed on the cliff. It was deliberately pushed off the cliff on to the beach, because excessive erosion threatened the safety of the structure.

Access to Mowhanau is along Kai Iwi Valley Road, 15 km west of Wanganui, or along Maxwell Station Road if coming from the west.

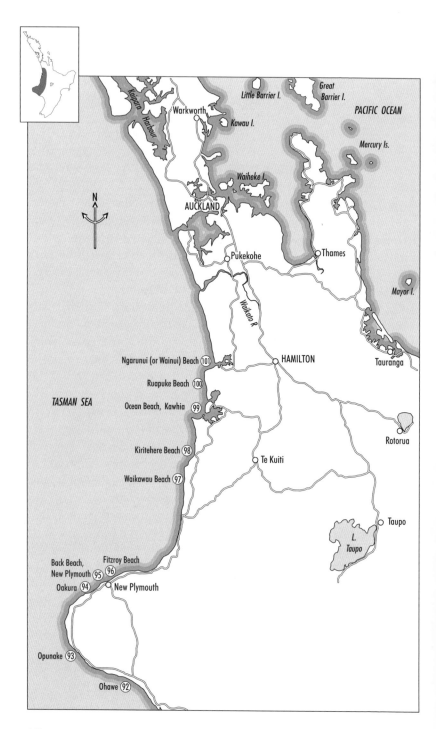

Kaipara Harbour

Little Barrier I.

Great Barrier I.

PACIFIC OCEAN

Warkworth

Kawau I.

Mercury Is.

Waiheke I.

N

AUCKLAND

Pukekohe

Thames

Mayor I.

Waikato R

TASMAN SEA

Ngarunui (or Wainui) Beach ⑩①

HAMILTON

Tauranga

Ruapuke Beach ⑩⓪

Ocean Beach, Kawhia ⑨⑨

Kiritehere Beach ⑨⑧

Te Kuiti

Rotorua

Waikawau Beach ⑨⑦

Taupo

Back Beach,
New Plymouth ⑨⑤

Fitzroy Beach ⑨⑥

L.
Taupo

Oakura ⑨④

New Plymouth

Opunake ⑨③

Ohawe ⑨②

# Taranaki

The semicircular form of Taranaki's coastline exposes its beaches to wind and waves from all directions. The black sands and rocky outcrops give the beaches a unique character. Dominated by the mighty Mount Taranaki, the coastline follows the arcing contour of the mountain's base.

Mount Taranaki pervades the whole atmosphere of the region, including the beaches. The clean, crisp mountain air tumbles from its slopes and the symmetrical form of the mountain provides a majestic backdrop to the beach vistas. The region boasts the possibility of snowboarding in the morning and surfing in the afternoon.

The exposure of the coastline to all westerly points of the compass and the reliable swell produced by the raging Tasman Sea makes the coastline a surfer's paradise. It is never far to drive to find good waves. Most beach towns such as Opunake and Oakura provide all the facilities surfers and beachgoers need. They form useful bases for further exploration of the region.

State Highway 45 circumnavigates the coastline and is dubbed the 'Surf Highway'. Most beaches are a short drive from the road. Many are accessible only by traversing private land.

Although sometimes showery, the region is graced by a mild climate, influenced, of course, by 'The Mountain'.

## Ohawe

Ohawe's days as a thriving beach town seem to have come to an end. The Surf Life Saving Club closed down in 1983 after 50 years' service, and most baches have been sold or turned into permanent residences.

The beach, however, is still pleasant, with spectacular cliffs rising 50 metres at the rear. The cliffs are banded with differing rock strata, including some fossil-rich layers. You need to take care exploring their base, as rock falls are frequent. Over the last 30–40 years, accelerated erosion of the cliffs has caused them to retreat up to 100 metres. Whenever chunks of rock fall off, interesting remnants usually materialise. Recent specimens included some human skulls.

Ohawe was the first site in New Zealand where moa bones were discovered. They were found in 1843 by Reverend Richard Taylor near hangi pits in the coastal dunes.

The beach is generally safe for swimming between the two lines of rock at right angles to the beach near the accessway. These were deliberately placed to provide protection for swimmers. There is also a popular freshwater swimming-hole approximately 100 metres up the Waingongoro River.

On the eastern side of the river mouth are the remains of a rusting winch, which was used to haul Maori fishing boats ashore in the late 1800s and early 1900s.

It is possible to launch boats at Ohawe. Parking is at the campground just above the beach, but seek permission first from the caretaker. There are nearby public toilets.

The Ohawe turn-off is signposted 6 km west of Hawera along Ohawe Road.

## Opunake

The striking and sheltered cove of Opunake Beach is immaculately presented and well cared for by the local community. They are rightfully proud of their attractive and quaintly proportioned beach. Opunake Beach is ringed by pohutukawa and low cliffs that lend a protected feel to the bay.

The black sand is diluted with lighter-coloured particles and shelves gently. It is sheltered by headlands on both sides, and swimming is safe in front of the Surf Life Saving Club towards the western end. Towards the eastern end there can sometimes be a rip.

Outflow from Opunake Lake is sometimes discharged into the bay and the impending rush of water is announced by a siren. The lake was formed in 1971 to feed the tiny power station under the cliff at the eastern end of the beach.

Opunake was a relatively isolated settlement until the late 1800s, when the first wharf was built on the western headland of Opunake Beach. The aim was to promote the town as the premier port of Taranaki. Stormy seas destroyed the wharf, and the second jetty, the remains of which are still visible today, was constantly pummelled by the sea, making mooring treacherous. Above Opunake Beach is a shipping marker constructed of four totara slabs bolted together. When lined up with a similar marker by the beach pavilion, ships at sea could be guided to the jetty.

The Opunake Walkway links all the main points of interest around the coastal part of the town, and you can walk various sections to reach the headlands at either side of the bay. Follow the walkway signs and markers. The cliffs are smothered in native vegetation, including flax, which used to be exported from the jetty.

The walk also links up with Middleton Bay, another sandy beach to the west. Although less attractive than Opunake Beach, it is good for walking the dog, as dogs are not allowed on Opunake Beach. The boat ramp for the town is at the eastern end of Middleton Bay.

The beach pavilion was built in 1931 and originally functioned as a tea-room. Also behind the beach are barbecues, picnic tables, public toilets, a children's play area and a campground. Community pride abounds in the well-kept area that services beach users.

Surfers flock to the area and use Opunake as a base for other beaches in the region. The most notable nearby spot is Kina Road, accessed along Kina Road, 10 km north of Opunake. Fishermen use the headland to catch kahawai and snapper.

Opunake has a full range of shops, accommodation and restaurants. The beach is signposted from SH45 and is accessed via Beach Road.

The secluded cove at Opunake is ringed by a walkway with magnificent coastal views.

## Oakura

From the moment you arrive in the vicinity of Oakura, you know it's a surfer's Mecca. Surfboard factories are housed in sheds on the outskirts, surfboards converted into postboxes ornament the roadsides and wetsuits are hung on any available fence. The world record for the most people on a surfboard was accomplished in Oakura. Fourteen people managed to stand on a moving board.

Oakura is the premier surf destination on the Taranaki coast. Surfers congregate here when conditions are right to surf the numerous breaks on and around the main beach area. The New Zealand Surfing Championships are held here occasionally. Ahu Bay at the southwestern end is the most popular area on Oakura Beach and is accessed via Ahuahu Road, just south of the town.

You can take a walk through the campground along a grass track to near Ahu Bay. The grass and metalled track passes a dune restoration project and a steep bank on the landward side is smothered in native coastal vegetation. The beach area here is rocky, so it is better to use the 1 km sandy stretch in front of Tasman Parade in the town.

The beach area has a shop, children's play area, parking, toilets, showers, changing sheds and Surf Life Saving Club. The beach is generally safe for swimming and shelves gently below the high-tide mark.

Boogie-boarders enjoy the waves away from the rocky area. Windsurfers and kite surfers take advantage of the prevailing westerly winds. Teenagers are well provided for with frequent good surf and a skate park near the beach. On New Year's Day the annual carnival attracts thousands of visitors to the entertainments on the beach.

Oakura has a boardriders club, campground on the beachfront and motels.

## Back Beach, New Plymouth

Back Beach looks out to the Sugar Loaf Islands Marine Protected Area, which was established in 1991 and aims to protect the area in its natural state. The towering rock of Paritutu stands sentinel at the northern end of the beach, with the imposing chimney of New Plymouth Power Station alongside. In the shadow of Paritutu is a fine stretch of sand barricaded by sheer cliffs of orange sandstone. You won't want to swim here as the water is very unsettled, but for scenic majesty and a refreshing walk it's a good location.

The Sugar Loaf Islands were named by Captain Cook in 1770, as they reminded him of the way sugar was stored in heaps or loaves. The islands harbour an abundance of aquatic and terrestrial life. Over 86 native plant species are recorded in the area and 80 fish species inhabit the fertile waters. The islands are best explored by boat. The closest boat ramp is near the lee breakwater inside Port Taranaki.

The best view of Back Beach is undoubtedly from the summit of Paritutu. This 30-minute-return climb is not for the faint-hearted. The track is extremely steep and slippery but climbers are aided by a cable bolted into the rocks. The start of the track is reached from the parking area near Paritutu Road off Centennial Drive.

For surfers the beach produces consistent waves on most tides.

To access Back Beach from the west, follow Beach Road from Omata until it turns into Centennial Drive. There is a parking area at the bottom of a dip in the hill. From central New Plymouth, head west along St Aubyn Street, which turns into Breakwater Road. Turn left into Ngamotu Road and immediately right into Centennial Drive. The parking area is after Rangitake Drive, which is on the right.

## Fitzroy Beach

Fitzroy Beach is the main beach for New Plymouth and is referred to by various names according to the particular part of the beach. At the western end it is sometimes called Strandon; the middle portion, Fitzroy; and near the river mouth, Waiwhakaiho.

The mouth of the Waiwhakaiho River is a good place to fish for kahawai. Surfcasters also catch snapper. The beach remains relatively clear of driftwood and is only inundated when the river is high from heavy rains on the northern slopes of Mt Taranaki.

The beach's biggest drawcard is its surf. It faces northwest and is best surfed in a northwesterly or westerly swell. The best spots vary with the direction of the swell, but generally the waves get bigger as you approach the Waiwhakaiho River. Boogie-boarders and windsurfers also enjoy the relatively consistent conditions. The beach is home to New Plymouth Boardriders Club Headquarters. At Easter, a surfmasters' championship is held for veteran surfers over 40.

The beach is patrolled by two Surf Life Saving Clubs and is generally safe for swimming. The Fitzroy Surf Life Saving Club has toilets and changing facilities. There is a campground, shop and paddling pool nearby. It is accessed from Beach Road, which is on the left heading east from the city along Devon Street.

At the western end of the beach is East End Surf Life Saving Club, approximately 500 metres from its Fitzroy counterpart. This is accessed via Nobs Line off Devon Street East. There is a skate park nearby. There are toilets, picnic facilities and grass reserves behind the beach.

The beach has a gentle curve and is bound by a promontory to the west and by a breakwater to the east at the mouth of the Waiwhakaiho River. In the distance to the west is Port Taranaki and the New Plymouth Power Station.

The New Plymouth Coastal Walkway links the urban coastal areas behind the beach and is well-marked.

# Waikato and King Country

Accessible beaches in the Waikato and King Country are not as plentiful as many other North Island regions. All the beaches exhibit the characteristic black sand typical of the west coast beaches.

Those beaches worth a visit have a raw and wild feel. There is majestic scenery and a humbling impression lingers with you after a visit. The coast is open to prevailing westerly winds and is the first land moisture–laden winds reach on their journey across the Tasman. In these conditions the beaches come into their own. The muted colours, wondrous vistas and atmospheric haze laden with salt spray lend a uniqueness to these beaches.

On sunny days the beaches are as good as any for traditional beach activities, but are also suitable for brisk walks to clear the head. Swimming can be dangerous, so seek local advice on some of the more exposed beaches.

Some, such as Ruapuke and Waikawau, are remote, with the drive to them being a part of the experience. Rolling farmland, tracts of native forest and secluded river valleys are enjoyable to explore on the way. The many tentacled arms of the harbours at Raglan and Kawhia separate the beaches and make for scenic drives between them.

Most Waikato and King Country beaches are far from settlements. It is best to come prepared.

## Waikawau Beach

The old stock tunnel is a startling entrance to the wild and dramatic beach at Waikawau. While walking through the tunnel the echoes of the breaking waves announce the nearby sea. The only window to the rolling waves is the arch at the seaward end.

Exiting the tunnel is like stepping into another world. Tufts of flax cling precariously to the sheer faces of the spectacular sandstone cliffs. The loose rock structure is etched with lines and hollows from wind and water weathering the crumbling strata.

The tunnel was constructed with picks and shovels by Jim Richard Scott, Charlie Christofferson and Bert Perrett. They were all employees of the Government Works Department. It was excavated wide enough for the widest horned beast and tall enough for the tallest horseman. The tunnel opened up the beach route for stock to reach the 4050-ha Nukuhakari Station. It was constructed because a steep bank formed an impenetrable barrier to the beach. Once the tunnel was completed, stock were driven to the beach and up the coast.

Children of early settlers used to play in the 50-metre-long tunnel and it was often smelly with a mixture of dung and water dripping from the ceiling to the floor channel. The floor can be wet and muddy, but you can usually pass through without getting your feet too dirty.

To the north of the tunnel, misty headlands recede to the horizon and, after periods of rain, waterfalls pour over the cliffs to the rocky shore below.

South of the tunnel are numerous sea caves, great for exploring and using as hideouts. Be careful of rockfalls from the cliffs. The black sand butts right up to the cliff base and is wide and clear of driftwood.

Waikawau Beach is 5 km along the signposted, unsealed Waikawau Beach Road. In places the road is very narrow, with extremely tight corners through the road cuttings. Watch for wandering stock on the road. There is a parking area and toilet by the tunnel.

Waikawau Beach Road is 33 km from Awakino and 33 km from Marokopa. Access from Awakino is along Manganui Road, which is 2 km east of the town. From Marokopa, follow Mangatoa Road. The winding road travels through native forest, pine plantations and farmland. The surface is only partly sealed.

## Kiritehere Beach

Kiritehere Beach lies at the wide mouth of a river valley surrounded by forest-covered hills. It's an isolated and wild black-sand beach that feels remote. Only a few small huts huddle behind the high dunes, but they are out of sight when you are on the beach.

North of the Kiritehere Stream is a parking area with a picnic table and basic toilet. There is also a fenced-off ancestral burial ground of the Tahi Hohaia Hikoia whanau. A track on the right leads over the dunes to the beach. Space on the beach here is limited, so it is better to cross the bridge over the Kiritehere Stream and use the other parking area.

This southern section of the beach is wide and slopes gently up to the sprawling tentacles of spinifex on the lower dunes. The sand is relatively free from driftwood, and at low tide a level shelf is exposed.

At the southern headland, rocks stretch around the coast and there are plenty of rock pools to fossick in. The sandstone is vibrantly coloured and crisscrossed with a mesmerising pattern of more resistant rock. The layers of deposited sediment that form the rock are clearly visible, and tilted to expose the strata.

To access Kiritehere Beach, head south from Marokopa for 5 km along Mangatoa Road and turn right into Soundy Road. Kiritehere Beach is a further 1.5 km.

## Ocean Beach, Kawhia

Ocean Beach is an open and exposed beach with views from the mouth of Kawhia Harbour all the way north to Mount Karioi. High dunes flank the rear portion of the beach and tongues of spinifex and marram creep down from the windswept tops. Dangerous rips extend all along the beach and swimming on the outgoing tide is especially ill-advised.

Like Hot Water Beach on the Coromandel, Ocean Beach is graced by upwelling springs of hot water, right on the beach. The springs here are less known and thus often less crowded than their Coromandel counterpart. Two hours either side of low tide you can dig your own spa in the sand and relax in an *au naturel* setting.

From the accessway over the dunes the main thermal area is more or less straight ahead. The exact location of the springs changes, but runs in a line roughly parallel to the water. To avoid wasted effort it is best to walk along the beach and at intervals sink your feet into the sand to sample the water temperature. If you encounter hot water, take your spade and dig.

While a spa at Ocean Beach is as relaxing as one at Hot Water Beach, the weather at Kawhia can be more fickle. The wind can be invigorating, and while you are submerged in your pool, poses little problem. However, if it is blowing with any strength, it can pick up the fine black sand and blast your eyes and face. Nevertheless, the experience of a private spa on the beach in wild surroundings is unsurpassable.

Ocean Beach is 5 km from Kawhia and well signposted from the town centre. There are toilets at the carpark. Kawhia has a range of accommodation and shops.

## Ruapuke Beach

Ruapuke is a raw and mystical beach, usually open to the ravages of the Tasman Sea. Its exposed black sands are fringed by steep pasture-covered hills, and headlands at both ends enclose the beach. The surf sometimes rolls in violently. There are rips and cross-currents. Surfers occasionally enjoy the waves in a southwesterly swell with offshore winds.

From the parking bay at the end of Ruapuke Beach Road, you will need to walk five minutes across the dunes. There is also a narrow, ankle-deep stream to cross, which is unavoidable.

There is a striking polarity of colour at Ruapuke. Driftwood is bleached white and many of the trunks exhibit their gnarled and twisted bases. The froth from the pounding surf is often picked up by the onshore wind and blown across the sand like globules of mercury. The further they retreat from the sea, the more diminished in size they become until they effervesce into nothingness. The white haze of salt spray lends a mystical atmosphere to the dramatic headlands and creates a surreal mood over the beach. This is a beach for walking along to blow the cobwebs away.

The beach is good for fishing, but the rocks at the northern headland are frequently battered by big waves and are dangerous to fish from. Find yourself a driftwood trunk to sit on and unpack your lunch while surfcasting.

Bleached shards of driftwood contrast with the black sand at Ruapuke.

From Raglan, turn left into Te Mata Road, 7 km east of the town along SH23. In Te Mata, turn into Ruapuke Road.

For a more hair-raising but scenic drive, follow Wainui Road past Whale Bay from Raglan. This turns into the unsealed Whaanga Road. Through many twists and turns, Whaanga Road climbs the western slopes of Mount Karioi, high above the Tasman Sea. Passing through kanuka forest and farmland, you reach the highlight of the trip, the precipitous Te Toto Gorge. Driving this route to Ruapuke enhances the impression of remoteness.

## Ngarunui (or Wainui) Beach

Raglan is *the* surf destination of New Zealand. Its consistent waves and distinguished boardriding history have made Raglan a place that oozes surf culture. The small town is packed with surf shops, and many other businesses use Raglan's reputation as a surfing Mecca to attract visitors.

Raglan was first surfed in the early 1960s by Peter Miller on a hollow 10-foot ply surfboard. After Raglan featured in the film *Endless Summer* (a surfing movie filmed by Bruce Brown that later reached cult status), many American and Australian surfers visited the beach to try the famous left-hand breaks. *Endless Summer 2* was filmed in the early 1990s and was based on the same scenario of two surf-crazy guys travelling the world in search of the ultimate wave. Raglan featured again, affirming its position as a world-class surf destination. Many over-60s still live and surf in Raglan.

Ngarunui is Raglan's main beach, 4 km west of the town and signposted along Wainui Road. Although not a surf beach, it looks out to 'The Point' further along the coast.

Manu Bay, as it is also known, is one of the best left-hand breaks in the country and if the water isn't full of surfers vying for position, then the carpark will be scattered with hopefuls waiting for the wind or swell direction to change. You can drive out along Wainui Road to the carpark and watch them catch waves.

The beach at Wainui stretches 2 km from the mouth of Raglan's harbour to a boulder bank at the southeastern end. There is less black sand here than beaches further south and has a bronze sheen. It's a wide and open beach, perfect for kite flying or blokarting.

At the western end, marram-covered dunes give way to steep hills smothered in flax and coastal scrub. The Waikato coast stretches north to the horizon, giving Ngarunui a dramatic setting. This is the last accessible beach north until the Waikato River mouth.

Approximately 100 metres east of the Surf Life Saving Club, a narrow but well-formed track leads from the bank behind the beach. This ten-minute one-way walk takes you to a lookout with views all the way up the beach and coastline.

The beach is patrolled by a Surf Life Saving Club near the tar-sealed accessway, but is prone to ever-changing rips and cross-currents. The carpark is a three-minute walk from the beach and is reached via Wainui Road. There is a basic toilet and changing shed on the beach. The beach is signposted through the Wainui Reserve.

At the roundabout in Wainui Reserve, both straight-ahead and left lead to the carpark. Choose right to access some lookouts above the beach. There are picnic tables, benches and toilets on the grass reserves. These are good spots for watching horse-riders on the beach, their dark silhouettes stark against the bright reflection of the shallow water at the harbour mouth.